FAITH OF A MUSTARD SEED

*Thoughts on the use of Faith
in The Gospels*

a compilation of columns written and published weekly in
The Nashville P*R*I*D*E

Barbara Woods Riles Washington, *M. Div.*

Faith Of A Mustard Seed
Thoughts on the use of Faith in The Gospels

Copyright © 2014 by **Barbara Woods Riles Washington**
All rights reserved

A compilation of columns written and published weekly in
The Nashville P*R*I*D*E
Nashville, Tennessee
March 23, 2007 - March 6, 2009

ISBN-13: 978-0-9913127-0-2

My Father's Mansion Press
PO Box 78605
Nashville TN 37207

Cover Art and Photograph by
Morgan B. Hines, DDS
PO Box 628
Columbia TN 38402

Lightning Source Inc.
1246 Heil Quaker Rd.
La Vergne, TN 37086

Another parable he put before them, saying, "The kingdom of heaven is like a grain of mustard seed which a man took and sowed in his field; it is the smallest of all seeds, but when it has grown it is the greatest of shrubs and becomes a tree..."
Matthew 13:31-32

And he said, "With what can we compare the kingdom of God, or what parable shall we use for it? It is like a grain of mustard seed, which, when sown upon the ground, is the smallest of all the seeds on earth; yet when it is sown it grows up and becomes the greatest of all shrubs, and puts forth large branches..."
Mark 4:30-33

He said therefore, "What is the kingdom of God like? And to what shall I compare it? It is like a grain of mustard seed which a man took and sowed in his garden; and it grew and became a tree..."
Luke 13:18-19

Dedication

This book is dedicated to the two people
who hold the most important threads of my hands:
my sister, Viola Woods Floyd
who is 'The Heart' of my family, and
my twin sister first cousin,
Jenice Golson Dunlap, a very special Lady.

and...

...always and forever
to the Spirit of our maternal grandmother
that has always kept us sound.

Ruth Magby Smith
1907 - 1972
Anniston Alabama - Cleveland Ohio

Foreword

Someone said recently, and I believe rightly so, that "stories" are what we take away from our experiences. The "stories," then become the threads, when woven together, that become the tapestry that is us. The volume that you now hold in your hand which represents an accumulation of "Mustard Seed Offerings" published over a number of years, provides a rare insight into how Barbara Woods Riles Washington came to be. Through the medium of anecdotes, close encounters of the most meaningful kind with people who left indelible impressions, scriptural exposition and application, and caveats that yield poignant lessons she emerges in full stature: powerful and direct, loving and patient, intellectual, loyal, spirit-filled, motivated, faithful!

In so many ways she is a Paul (Pauline?). Among folk for whom credentials (confidence in the flesh) were essential, Paul could point to his lineage, his training, and his sterling reputation – "touching righteousness which is in the Law, blameless." But what things were gain to him, those he counted loss for Christ (Philippians 3: 4 – 11). Barbara has spent her life subordinating her credentials, acquaintances and exposure to her passion for the excellency of the knowledge of Christ Jesus (her) Lord, that she strives to win.

Clement W. Fugh
Presiding Bishop
African Methodist Episcopal Church

The Nashville P*R*I*D*E (Positive, Relevant, Information, Devoted to Education), "The Voice of a Proud Community," began to lay it's foundation in the latter part of 1987 when Dr. Larry Davis shared his vision of a black owned and operated weekly newspaper with Dr. Cynthia Hodge. Thus, the beginning of the Nashville PRIDE, dba, Pride Publishing Group, Inc., with D.D. Drico, a holding company as it's initial funding source.

The company used as its birth date The Martin Luther King, Jr.'s Birthday Celebration and March held on the 15th of January, 1988. On that day hundreds of the first issue of the Nashville PRIDE were sold for 25 cents each at the MLK March; and the doors of the new office on Jefferson Street in the Frierson Building, were also opened for business.

My tenure with the company, as managing editor, began during the third issue of the publication, under the supervision of the co-publishers Drs. Davis and Hodge, the founders. Under the leadership of Dr. Davis the corporation grew over the years, developing eight newspapers, that had begun with the parent paper and anchor, the Nashville PRIDE, followed by: the Chattanooga Courier, the Clarksville Press, the Knoxville Enlightener, and the Murfreesboro Vision, of Tennessee. The three other newspapers, now defunct, were in Ohio, South Carolina, and Alabama. Presently, the Nashville PRIDE and the four other papers in Tennessee are still being published. The Editor at that time and still is a "ghost" editor, Cynthia Aileen Lydia.

Now in it's 25th Year, the Pride corporation continues under the leadership of Dr. Davis' sons, Meekahl Davis, President/CEO and co-publisher and Navada Scott Davis, vice president in charge of advertising sales and circulation, also co-publisher. The Nashville PRIDE "stars" over the years have been the writers, who have told the positive stories in the African American community as well as the stories that impact the community. The most consistent "stars" and the most recognizable have been our columnists, religious as well as secular, who have shared their expertise with our readers.

We are proud to share the information of the PRIDE history with one of our long-running columnists, the Rev. Barbara Woods Washington. The Reverend Barbara, who I am delighted to call a friend, is not only skilled in the oral delivery and writing of the "Word of God," but is one of the mostgifted, creative people that I have ever known - with hands that are magical when it comes to quilting, scrap-booking, sewing, and much more.

A comment from one of her column readers shared, "Rev. Barbara often gives an unexpected slant on the interpretation of the word." We are very proud that she had chosen to publish her columns that bring insight and joy to so many.

Geraldine D. Heath
Managing Editor
Nashville P*R*I*D*E

Introduction

I am a product of the Sunday School of the 1950s Black Church religious culture. I love looking at pictures taken in front of the Church from that era which have what looks like a gazillion children standing so closely knit that faces must be magnified in order to identify them. I inherited one such picture from my birth Church when we were located on Cedar Avenue in Cleveland, Ohio. Looking into this picture I can see all of my brothers and sisters. Has the "training up of a child..." been lost on the Black Church? Now, in 2013, I have come into the realization that the Sunday School IS my Church. While I am not currently teaching Bible Study, I have found a class that works The Word of God "...in the ways that they ought to go...", —no pre-formatted curriculums— just a simple 'free thinking', 'life application' walk through The Bible.

In March 2007 I began this journey of writing a weekly column for the **Nashville P*R*I*D*E** Newspaper. At the time, I knew that I wanted to write concerning Faith and from the outset took the title "***Faith Of A Mustard Seed***" which has remained to date. This coming together of writings for the P*R*I*D*E is a response to several requests. It is purposed for provoking thought among groups that have gathered to study Bible with Life emphasis. It is my prayer that it might inspire someone to initiate groups of persons to come together to Study Bible in some new way and light.

It begins with a personal statement of my life journey. "While working at Grady Hospital in Atlanta, GA, 'I heard a cry' or did 'He hear my cry'?" To the statement written from Dr. Howard Thurman as scholarship invitation during my first year in Seminary —"I am pleased to extend to you on behalf of the Howard Thurman Educational Trust an invitation to participate in a seven day intensive seminar discussion with me on the grounds and the meaning of religious experience." To this statement drawn from the experience of teaching Philosophy of Religion at Bennett College to young women whom I soon realized were in the first public religion course of their lives —"How do we affect the ever changing global community when our personal Church traditions (as smug as so many of them are) is all that we bring?"

Drawing upon the biblical and historical Faith dialogue as it began to emerge in this column this statement is made: —"Far to many lives give over their God given powers and spiritual gifts to others without ever having emerged an 'articulate self'." Then as the discussion follows the 'Four Components of Theology' this statement is made: —"The experience question must include the 'human predicament' which has as a vital part the fact of our experiencing the world from 'inside out'. The individual, 'I am' the center of the universe in that we are stuck in this body. We see 'out' of our eyes". Thus Jesus' FIRST demand for discipleship: —"if any man will come after me, let him deny himself...".

The discussion enters Bible with this discovery —"the New Testament's first reference to WORD is also the first reference to FAITH!" "All Jesus had was 'His Word' which as he spoke to persons of sufferance, they began to follow him around. And yet, he never used the means of those who followed him to alter his 'homeless existence'; which, I think, is a very vital part of the power of 'His Word'! He never took anything from his followers! To be sure, he charged his disciples to *"take nothing..."* Word-'logos' and Faith-'pistis'. WORD AS FAITH!" Methodology now appears. "Of the numerous words for Faith in the Greek New Testament, 'pistis' is used most often, almost solely in the Gospels, by Jesus. Now, to look at each occurrence of this word as a walk through the Bible.

These thoughts emerge: —"Sickness, I suspect, is the most humbling experience of a life. The most cheerful life; the most prideful and arrogant; the atheist, the wealthiest; the most disinherited life— all experience a transition in both personality and character when affliction comes." And this statement: —"Many of the most radical sayings that place Jesus in direct conflict with those things that were established in both the religious and national life were pronounced as a direct result of the probing and questioning of the Scribes." And this statement: —"Jesus' use of the word 'egeiro/rise' in the 'Healing of The Paralytic' faith event is a perfect command that can only be given by God. The hearer must carry out the command as though his life depends upon it."

As the discussion on Jesus' use of Faith continues the 'Epileptic Boy Healed' faith event invokes this thought: —"It occurs to me that the limited capabilities that we as humans have in the use of the 'rebuke command', is directly related to motive. Double-mindedness, hidden agendas and the like have rendered the modern disciple of Jesus great personal gain at the expense of a 'demon controlled' church. *"Why could we not cast it out?"* The 'unclean heart' cannot affect an 'unclean spirit'." To this thought: —"Much talk about how many Christians who worship with a high level of commitment, leave the church Sunday after Sunday without ever having experienced any 'God given attention' to our diseases." Then to this: —"Christians go from Church to Church, seeking, looking for healing from diseases and infirmities, turning over resources to 'disciples' who gain wealth and lay up treasures on earth.' *"Why could we not cast it out?"*

As the discussion moves further into the 'Epileptic Boy Healed' faith event the Disciples concern for their inability to 'exorcize' authority over 'unclean spirits' invoked Jesus' response being —"'Oligo pistian' = 'little faith'. Spiritual healing powerlessness directly related to 'little faith'. Jesus used one of the 'littlest seeds' to teach his disciples about the measure of faith. Your faith is little— look at this little seed!" Then this revelation —"There is no usage of 'mustard seed' in the Old Testament. Biblically, it is found only 5 times— all 5 usages exclusive to Jesus. The 5 becomes 2 as this teaching to measure faith by the 'mustard seed' is a double tradition (Matthew 17:20) and (Luke 17:6);"

Significant to the dialogues on Faith is the work of Paul Tillich. His thought is introduced with these statements: —"The Church and it's servants," Tillich suggests, (have made the Word From The Lord) "a matter of law and tradition, of habit and convention. A possession. That no longer cuts into 'our ordinary world'. A possession. Of something that can NEVER BE possessed! Ceasing to ask and to cry out for It... IS THERE ANY WORD FROM THE LORD?" And: —"Noting the long struggle that the historical Church had with 'seeing and hearing', the homily now recognizes that 'hearing' won the battle during the Reformation when the Church became centered around the 'preacher's desk'— "Hearing replaced seeing, obedience replaced vision." Most significant for me is this statement— "Seeing is the most astonishing of our natural powers. It receives the light, the first of all that is created, and as the light does it conquers darkness and chaos."

This is an invitation to enter into the weekly thoughts on Faith that have approached the dialogue on the 'Four Gospels' use of Faith/pistis in the mouth and ministry of Jesus of Nazareth. As a final invocation in these writings, I submit a personal statement concerning the 'First' and perhaps most convictional faith event teaching of Jesus, 'The Centurion's Boy' or 'The Centurion's Slave': —"With no known interracial marriages in the five generational blood line that I have traced back to Magby slave ownership in Newnan, Coweta County, Georgia, I am still unable to account for the 'whiteness' of my family's skin, with some of my great and great great grand nieces and nephews being born 'white as cotton'? America has asked us 'to forget about' the centurion's (the master) decreeing himself the right to go in and out of our mother's most private life 'depositing seeds' that he would 'own' but never 'give kinship'. Whom he would 'capitalize on' but never 'be familial'. America wants to 'label', 'rebuke' and 'shun' the 'mad black woman' with no accountability for it's birthing of the 'mad black woman'! Now they say 'get over it'! How do you get over an 'absentee father' who IS A CENTURION?"

Barbara Woods Riles Washington, M. Div.
Nashville, Tennessee
December 2013

Acknowledgement

The thanks are far too many to count. Only God knows the influences that persons of trust have given to my life journey. To my maternal grandmother, my second parent, Ruth Magby Smith— the 'beatings'; the corn rowing; the proper way to make a bed at her day work in Mrs. Whitehead's house; the crocheting and knitting; the psalms; the Salvation Army and all of it's ministries; the quilting at our Church when we became the Glenville Church of God; the love in her eyes when I made my way to this Church on Sunday during my turbulent High School years...

My teachers, Ed Landers; Patricia Ackerman; Lelia McBath. Dr. Major J. Jones who told me when I entered Seminary, "go to Central Church Sunday, join, and tell Dr. Lowery that you are a new student at Gammon." Dr. Bishop Thomas Hoyt and Dr. John Waters for lighting a fire for Bible that ever burns eternal.

Thanks goes out on many avenues, a wide range of family and friends who I asked to assist in the editing of these columns. It was with a purposeful heart that very few changes were made from the original P*R*I*D*E publications. The single quotation marks are retained as style and used throughout most often to indicate a topic for further study. Where there are two numbers on a page, the one with the Cross is the Column number in the order written.

More thanks to the man that I married Lorenzo Washington who has shown a light of true manhood in a life where this was void; and to his partner and my friend, Dr. Morgan B. Hines. I give thanks to God always for the gift of your friendship.

A world of gratitude to a very special, God-given entity in my Nashville existence, Evelyn Suggs.

Faith of a mustard seed
by Barbara Woods-Washington, M. Div.

I was born in Cleveland, OH where my mother, as head of the household, at one time during my childhood cared for seven of her own children; six grandchildren; her mother; a sister and her husband and two children; a niece and her three children. Count them, that makes 23 family members all living on the 2nd floor (and attic) of a two family house. As an elementary school student, my responsibilities as my grandmother's 'right hand' in the daily provisions for the babies, gave rise to a powerful mission in ministry to children.

After graduating from John F. Kennedy High School, I am the first in my family to 'ship off to college'. In the fall of 1970, I found myself as a freshman in WRC Hall at Tennessee State University. Shortly after graduating from TSU I followed the 'notoriety' of a city that I kept hearing so much about, Atlanta, GA.

While working at Grady Hospital, 'I heard a cry' or did 'He

Barbara Woods Riles Washington

hear my cry'? But, in a thirty day or so time span, I was enrolled in the summer session to begin a three year Master of Divinity degree program at Gammon Theological Seminary of the Interdenominational Theological Center. Hadn't been to church since leaving home seven years earlier, and now my whole world had been made brand new. At the time, I couldn't even spell seminary, inter-denominational or theology, let alone know what they meant. To complete this 3 year course, I also found myself sitting in the pulpit of Central United Methodist Church at a time when Dr. Joseph Lowery was at the height of his leadership as President of the Southern Christian Leadership Conference. He told me my 2nd Sunday there, "reach in the closet and get a robe, grab a Bible and read..." I said "huh"?? (I did tell you that I hadn't been to church in 7 years?) He said, "what part don't you understand, robe? Bible?" Again I said,

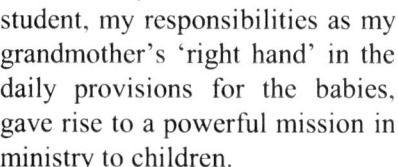

The Voice Of A Proud Community
Nashville P*R*I*D*E
Pulpit, Pew and Public

"huh"??? He said, "you gon be a preacher or you gon be a chicken?"

My first pastorate after graduating was the appointment to Gordon Road UMC then located on MLK Jr. Dr. just past the Westview Cemetery. Three years of ministry that remains very close to my heart as the families of this church community continue to remind me of the life and labors of love we shared in Christ. I left Gordon Road in 1984 for Drew University in Madison, NJ. As a PhD candidate in Biblical Studies, I chose to major in New Testament with The Parables as my area of dissertation. I had identified the 'Parables With Private Interpretation' and began to research the three found in Mark's Gospel. I studied both biblical languages on my masters level which was a requirement for entrance into this program; but, my first semester language study was now German.

While at Drew, I was contacted by two District Superintendents: in New Jersey and New York. I met the Pastor Parish Committee of the Gladstone Peapack UMC (NJ) on a Friday Night and that Sunday, I preached the morning service at Bethel in Brooklyn. By Monday, I had received a unanimous vote from both congregation's Pastor Parish committee and returned the following Sunday as Pastor to Bethel UMC in the 'Bedford-Stuyvesant' community of Brooklyn, NYC. After my first Charge Conference at Bethel, I was summoned to Riverside Drive's **'God Box'** to a meeting with some very important men who had put a package together to purchase a former bank building which they wanted me to use in developing a new church congregation. The location was Jamaica Queens in the same community as Allen AME Church which was for me, 'THE MODEL' for church. I didn't think long before I received a call from the Rev. Dr. T. P. Grissom, Jr., inviting me to serve as his Associate at Salem, in Harlem. I still long to hear the Chancel Choir singing *'Come unto Jesus, while you have time'* in procession to the communion table. And Good Friday at Salem... nothing like it... anywhere!

In my third year at Salem, Dr. Gloria Scott was the Black College Fund Banquet speaker. She was among the distinguished guests who had visited Gordon Road during my pastorate. When I went up to greet her, she said "I've been looking for you." In July 1988 I became the first woman to serve as Chaplain to Bennett College in Greensboro. Taught Philosophy of Religion. But my **Belles of Harmony Gospel Choir**, which I took on three choir tours is what *'I Never Shall Forget!'*■

*An Invitation to Study Bible Thursdays. 6:30 pm
mustardseedfaith@bellsouth.net*

March 23, 2007

Faith of a mustard seed
by Barbara Woods-Washington, M. Div.

On 9-11 in 1979, Howard Thurman posted a letter to me during my second year in Seminary. "I am pleased", he wrote, "to extend to you on behalf of the **Howard Thurman Educational Trust** an invitation to participate in a seven day intensive seminar discussion with me on the grounds and the meaning of religious experience."

I had been raised in the Church of God where worship was not just at the eleven o'clock hour every Sunday, but also at 7:30 pm. (I understood clearly when my PhD New Testament class studies on Paul's Law In Romans challenged me to 'de-mythologize grandmother' because) from Sunday school through evening service, every Sunday, my grandmother kept me at church all day, so I 'knew church'.

Barbara Woods Riles Washington

During the week, I remember attending various services at so many different churches in and out of our community. Temple Baptist on Cedar Avenue where the choir would come down the aisle singing "We've come this far by faith, leaning on the Lord, trusting in His holy word, He's never failed me yet, Oh, oh oh oh, can't turn around...". And the Sanctified store front church on Central near our corner, 76th street where the door always stood open; summoning the frequent visitors to Pappy's Bar next door; as the praise was fearful for me: "I'm a soldier, in the army of the Lord, I'm a soldier in the army. I'm fighting for my life, in the army of the Lord..". The Watch Night services at the Salvation Army on the corner of our street; so I 'knew tradition'.

"The Voice Of A Proud Community"
Nashville P*R*I*D*E
Pulpit, Pew and Public

But the grounds, and the meaning, of Religious Experience???, this was a whole other matter! Dr. Thurman wrote further to me saying, "You will be one of ten young people from different sections of the United States. All of whom have two things in common: (1) The "nerve center of consent" has been given to the religious life as a personal commitment and (2) each one is Black."

And so we gathered in San Francisco, the ten of us, two doctorals, six seminarians, and two undergraduates for a week of discussions along the line of his statement in **"Jesus And The Disinherited"**■

An Invitation to Study Bible
Thursdays. 6:30 pm
mustardseedfaith@bellsouth.net

March 30, 2007

Faith of a mustard seed
by Barbara Woods-Washington, M. Div.

In his **'Epilogue'** to **'Jesus And The Disinherited'**, Dr. Howard Thurman has managed to give critical direction and purpose to life in these words: "When a solitary individual is able to mingle his strength with the forces of history and emerge with a name, a character, a personality,... it means that against the background of anonymity he has emerged articulate... ". In defining a major point of departure for Bible-Life Study, I am convinced that the concept 'articulate' must be examined.

I recall my year at Boston University in 1971-72 and the fact that in my movement through the city's public transportation system to and from campus to my work study job teaching sewing at the Harriet Tubman House on Holyoke St., I was plagued by brothers who, in their zealousness for the Black Muslim faith in which they had found deliverance, hurled at me doctrines which were disturbing to me at the time. It was not a question of 'smugness' for I had not darkened the door of a single church in Boston. But, I suspect, a question of 'articulation of faith'.

Later in my life while in ministry at Salem, in Harlem, I was making hospital rounds and stopped in a clothing store on Delancy Street. The Jewish shop owner looked at the clergy collar that I was wearing and began to question me about my faith. His questions went to the very heart, the very gut of Christianity. The kind of questions that make for warfare in the Bible Study classes of the traditional Church! By the time I broke away we had spent over two hours in dialogue

Barbara Woods Riles Washington

"The Voice Of A Proud Community"
Nashville P*R*I*D*E
Pulpit, Pew and Public

and he said to me that I was the most intelligent Christian that he had met. At first I thought this to be quite an honor. But, the more I think about it, how many Christians had ever spent the time with him, (or any Jewish fellow) on the grounds and meaning of our belief system? I knew then that I was learning to articulate my faith. Time and time again I came to know in the streets of New York City that a troubled life is stopped in it's tracks in the midst of an articulate faith statement.

When I began teaching Philosophy of Religion at Bennett College, I came to terms with the demonic environment that Christian/religious education settings breed. As I began to develop the skill for diffusing the condemnation, in order that each could be free to express their faith views without fear of attack, I soon realized that this was for the vast majority of college aged students, the very first public religious education environment. How do we affect the ever changing global community when our personal Church traditions (as smug as so many of them are) is all that we bring? ■

An Invitation to Study Bible Thursdays. 6:30 pm mustardseedfaith@bellsouth.net

April 6, 2007

Faith of a mustard seed
by Barbara Woods-Washington, M. Div.

In the 'articulation of faith' process, one must come to terms with *'word'*. ('Word' as I prematurely refer to the familiar 'New Genesis' as John's Gospel proclaims in Chapter 1, verse 1: *"In the beginning was the Word..."*; but far to early here to take this leap of faith). And so I enter the text first, at Matthew's use of 'logos/word'.

Barbara Woods Riles Washington

Young's Concordance identifies 14 uses of 'logos' in Matthew's Gospel that upon closer look definitively places 'word' within the context of faith. First, the reference to the 'logos of Jesus' and it's power for healing; separate even from his presence— but only by 'His Word'. The Centurion said, (8:8), you (Jesus) don't have to come to my house where my sick servant is, just speak a word of healing.... But he was not the only one who knew about the power of 'Jesus' logos', for Matthew's 2nd use (8:16) records that many brought their demon possessed loved ones, and by 'His Logos'... By Matthew's 3rd use of Word, it is now in reference to the 'Disciple's logos' (10:14) when Jesus admonished them that if their 'logos' is not received, shake the dust off and move on to the next town.

It is no small thing that 'logos/word' is compounded with most every area of life to give definition to how and what we learn to think. Bio-logos, biology, my word, my study, my thinking is in terms of the physical human life, even to be distinguished from zoo-logy. My word could be Psyche-logos, cardiology; thanatology; even eulogy.

If I see, talk, think in terms of disease causation and treatment, my word would be

'The Voice Of A Proud Community'
Nashville P*R*I*D*E
Pulpit, Pew and Public

aetiology. Anthropology; astrology; demonology threatens the very infrastructure of Christianity. Cynology—doghood, dogkind; dentrology—treehood, treekind. Musicology; mythology; Christology. A list so long that persons are dedicating life study to compilations of logies as a discipline in and of itself. My personal list currently includes 192 logy disciplines that I believe to be crucial knowledge in my understanding and 'articulation of faith—my Theology!' It is true: "God Specializes!" ■

An Invitation to Study Bible Thursdays, 6:30 pm mustardseedfaith@bellsouth.net

April 13, 2007

Faith of a mustard seed
by Barbara Woods-Washington, M. Div.

'Theos/God'-'logos/word'—theology: God-word; God-study; God-thinking, as a discipline gives rise to the 'self examined life' in order to give understanding to the ways and presence of God both universally and historically.

Systematic Theology has identified four major components to the individual theology:
1) scripture,
2) tradition,
3) sources and
4) experience.

The order is not definitive and changes with each theologian. Upon further examination of the components, it is clear to me that each individual has the task of developing his/her own theology based upon a fact of genius in the 'Creating Hand of God' in making each one uniquely different! Traditionally, we have appointed religious leaders to do our theologies for us. We think what they think, we do what they tell us to do. Subsequently, far to many lives give over their God given powers and spiritual gifts to others without ever having emerged an 'articulate self'.

Barbara Woods Riles Washington

First in the order for me is Sources. As a New Testament scholar, the field of Source Criticism in Biblical Studies is most intriguing to me. But, for the self examined life in the articulation of faith process, one must begin by coming to terms with the weighty issue of one's own sources.

It is no small thing that 'psyche/mind' - 'logos/word'—psychology; psychiatric treatment of the troubled personality generally begins by taking the life back to it's earliest memories, for mother is the primary source of any life.

"The Voice Of A Proud Community"
Nashville P*R*I*D*E
Pulpit, Pew and Public

While I was in ministry at Salem, the United Methodist Women had a ministry to the crack born babies at Harlem Hospital where they simply went to the Neo-Natal Unit and sat in rocking chairs holding the infant. If you would hold in your hands a new born life whose mother had transmitted a crack cocaine addiction in the womb, you would cry too, as they do— uncontrollably!

Our sources expand to include our father, siblings, extended family; pastors and teachers. Barbara Bush quoted Fulghum in her commencement address at Wellesley in saying "All I really need to know, I learned in Kindergarten". I thought that I had a good teacher in Edward Landers, 5th grade at Quincy Elementary and Patricia Ackerman, 9th grade at FDR Jr.High. And then I met Lelia McBath in the 10th grade at JFK.

Our sources go beyond the books we read to identify those writers, (for me) like Howard Thurman, James Cone, James Weldon Johnson, Rudolph Bultmann, etc., whose writings you don't stop until you own and have digested everything that they have written. ■

An Invitation to Study Bible Thursdays. 6:30 pm
mustardseedfaith@bellsouth.net

April 20, 2007

Faith of a mustard seed
by Barbara Woods-Washington, M. Div.

In my theology, as it is a lifelong continuum— I see the logical progression from sources to scripture.

I recall early in my childhood my grandmother was a missionary of our church (among her many church works— she had a key!). But she made me learn to recite scripture and took me with her to visit the sick. I learned Psalms 1; 23; 24; 27; 121 and 150 among others that, unlike these, remain printed on my heart.

When I think scripture, I think of my Old Testament History professor, Dr. John Waters who studied seven languages with dissertation in Assyriology. Also my New Testament History professor, Dr. Thomas Hoyt who is now a Bishop in the C.M.E. Church. Together, these two men have developed my understanding of scripture to achieve a year of PhD work in Biblical Studies.

Initially, my discussion of scripture pivots upon translation— the Revised Standard Version used by both these Biblical Scholars as their teaching tool, as did Dr. G.Murray Branch, my Old Testament Literature professor, who came to class with only his grade book and the Oxford Annotated RSV and called the roll at 8:00 am on the dot.

When I think scripture, I think of the Documentary produced on Dr. Howard Thurman; and of his response to the question: if the Bible were taken away, what book would he keep. He replied, The **'139th Psalm'**. In considering how I would respond, again and again my word continues to return to **'John 5'**. (Shout out to one of my Bennett College Students,

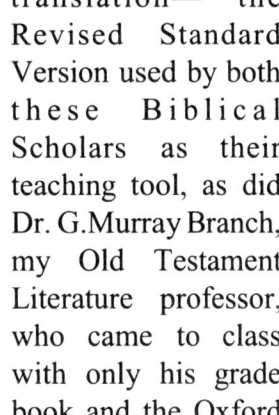

Barbara Woods Riles Washington

☦ 6

"The Voice Of A Proud Community"
Nashville P*R*I*D*E
Pulpit, Pew and Public

Da'Mica Wilson O'Bryant). I used the John 5 text in facilitating the workshop: **'Addiction: A Religious Perspective'** for the **2003** annual conference of the **Indiana Criminal Justice Institute, Governor's Commission for a Drug-Free Indiana** for which she served as Planning Chair. For this event, I saw the porticoes of Bethzatha as a place of addiction.

When I think scripture, I recall the 3-Night Revival that I preached at Mitchell Chapel/St. Luke Charge in Ashboro, NC while at Bennett, where through the conversation in the Pastor's study the first night, I heard a voice sing "The Lord, He Is, My Shepherd! 3 times! ... And I shall not want!" I had the need to leave the study joining the service of Devotion. The 2nd verse said, "He feeds me, when, I'm hungry! 3 times!... And I shall not want!" Unadulterated scripture... that 23rd Psalm is!.■

An Invitation to Study Bible Thursdays, 6:30 pm
mustardseedfaith@bellsouth.net

April 27, 2007

Faith of a mustard seed
by Barbara Woods-Washington, M. Div.

Barbara Woods Riles Washington

Tradition, I suspect to be the most difficult of the four components that the systematic theologian looks at in defining faith. Not simply because of the innumerable denominations in which the Christian faith has splintered; not even because of the unaccounted for number of churches that exist. I have yet to notice a four-corner Church location, but in every town in which I have lived, I can identify a 'three corner Church'. In Nashville, one is the very glaring location of Highway 70 and Cross Timbers Dr. where on one corner is the Bellevue Church of Christ. Cross the street to the second corner to Bellevue Baptist Church. Then cross the street to the third corner to Bellevue Presbyterian Church.

I matriculated at the Interdenominational Theological Center during the time when Absalom Jones Seminary of the Episcopal Church was closing it's doors in the ITC, opting for their St. Augustine location in Raleigh, NC. The constituent Seminaries then went from seven to six by the time of my graduation in 1981. In alpha order, students prepare for ministry in the African Methodist Episcopal Church (Turner Theological Seminary); the Baptist Church (Morehouse School of Religion); the Christian Methodist Episcopal Church (Phillips School of Theology); the Church of God In Christ (Charles H. Mason Theological Seminary); the Presbyterian Church (Johnson C. Smith Theological Seminary; and the United Methodist Church (Gammon Theological Seminary). The six Church traditions study the entire

"The Voice Of A Proud Community"
Nashville P*R*I*D*E
Pulpit, Pew and Public

✝ 7

theological curriculum together for a common foundation in the Christian faith with the single exception of two courses prescribed for maintaining the separate traditions: (mine United Methodist) Church History; and Church Polity. In my discussion of Experience, I credit the common foundation received at the ITC as one of the most important experiences of my life.

In this short space, I am reminded of a life long member of Salem who at her passing, we were required to hold her services at the Kingdom Hall because her daughter's church tradition became more important than her mother being buried from the Church in which she herself had chosen to live her religious life. More recently when I went to Los Angeles to participate in the funeral services for Harry McBath at Knox Presbyterian Church, I held a conversation with his nephew who was clear about his commitment to the Jehovah Witness tradition when I asked if he was allowed to be here at this Church? He replied "My Uncle Harry is far more important to me."■

An Invitation to Study Bible Thursdays. 6:30 pm mustardseedfaith@bellsouth.net

May 4, 2007

Faith of a mustard seed
by Barbara Woods-Washington, M. Div.

Experience as a component of theology is, I think, the grounding factor. The places, the spaces, the faces of any life, both as an individual or as a part of one's total historicity will ultimately alter any source or tradition.

It has always been interesting to me to hear persons appeal to their experience in stating their point of view: "Live long enough and you will know!" "I'm not telling you what I read, I'm telling you what I know!" "I've been all over the world and I've seen it time and time again!" My mother's sister, Mama Lodie, with only a junior high school level education to speak of, was one of the smartest women I have known in my lifetime. She called it 'common sense'. My mother's brother, Uncle Buddy taught me to play a card game called 'Coon' when I was very young. He said, among other things, "cooning and schooling". Later in my life while riding Amtrak between New York and Atlanta, I met a man in the club car who will never forget that I 'cooned him' the entire trip while folks watched and marveled! Experience really is the best teacher.

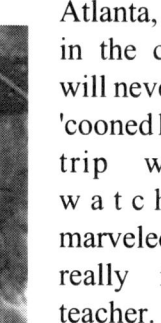

Barbara Woods Riles Washington

The experience question must include the 'human predicament' which has as a vital part the fact of our experiencing the world from 'inside out'. The individual, 'I am' the center of the universe in that we are stuck in this body. We see 'out' of our eyes (at best those things in front of me, never behind my back). The event is real for me only if 'I am' present. It is no small thing that the very first criteria for faith, as Jesus puts it, *"If anyone would come after me... deny self..."*

"The Voice Of A Proud Community"
Nashville P*R*I*D*E
Pulpit, Pew and Public

✝ 8

Experience is it's own knowledge base. To be sure it is the participation in the event, the exposure, the involvement that determines the knowledge or skill gained in the experience.

When you consider the fact that the African's birthright as American was defined in a context where education was outlawed, the assimilation of culture was only by experience.

The value of experience is now being recognized by Colleges and Universities in their offering of credits and programs in Life Experience. We not only experience life mentally and physically, but also emotionally and spiritually.

No discussion of experience in the context of systematic theology could be complete without an introduction to the work of Paul Tillich. He identifies two poles which he thinks that theology must move back and forth between: eternal truth and temporal situation. It is the creative interpretation of experience that is critical.■

An Invitation to Study Bible
Thursdays, 6:30 pm
mustardseedfaith@bellsouth.net

May 11, 2007

Faith of a mustard seed
by Barbara Woods-Washington, M. Div.

My column of April 13th was the second one that went through an editing hand that caused confusion for me. Particularly since the changes made altered drastically the thesis of the writing. In my defense of these things I wrote, "Talking To The Hand" and so far so good. I say this here only because, as God would have it, the direction given this column has returned to the April 13th writing. I wrote:—

[In the 'articulation of faith' process, one must come to terms with "word". (Word as I prematurely refer to the familiar "New Genesis" as John's Gospel proclaims in Chapter 1, verse 1: "In the beginning was the Word..."; but far to early here to take this leap of faith). And so I enter the text first, at Matthew's use of 'logos/word'.]

What you read was a different thesis statement simply

Barbara Woods Riles Washington

by 'the hand's' injection of <u>THE</u> in front of my initial use of WORD. The parenthesis was taken away by 'the hand' along with other changes, but these two most critical.

First, one must come to terms with WORD. I am intentionally not putting a qualifier in order to speak to all listeners, no matter whether you are within any faith context or not, most specifically, not bound by age. I am reminded of the pop to hip hop culture use of WORD. One very popular song's hook simply said "Word Up, tell me what's the word? Word Up!" Another rap refrain required an affirmation in it's participation with the listeners: "Word Up—Hey! Word Up—Hey! For real 'tho!" Even to the point where in my work with youth in ministry, many of

† 9

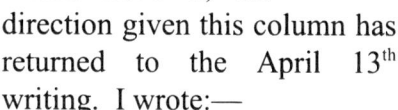

"The Voice Of A Proud Community"
Nashville P*R*I*D*E
Pulpit, Pew and Public

them had adopted WORD as their affirmation and you could hear them responding throughout their dialogue time and time again with just— 'WORD'!

Once this is recognized, then and only then, do I speak of a qualifying Word which I put in parenthesis as an aside indicating that it is far to early to take this leap of faith. 'The hand' removed my parenthesis and needless to say, my entire thesis suffered loss. What then am I saying? If a qualifier must be put to WORD, try (YOUR) WORD! In the articulation of faith process one must come to terms with (one's) WORD! It is true—"your WORD IS your bond!" I wrote: —

[Young's Concordance identifies 14 uses of logos in Matthew's Gospel that upon closer look definitively places 'word' within the context of faith. First, the reference to the 'logos of Jesus' and it's power for healing; separate even from his presence, but only by His Word. The Centurion said, (8:8), you (Jesus) don't have to come to my house where my sick servant is, just speak a word of healing...]. You read, again 'the hand'.

The true revelation in returning to the April 13th column lies in the fact that the New Testament's first reference to WORD is also the first reference to FAITH! Time now to take a closer look at "THE CENTURION'S SERVANT". ■

An Invitation to Study Bible Thursdays, 6:30 pm mustardseedfaith@bellsouth.net

---
May 18, 2007

Faith of a mustard seed
by Barbara Woods-Washington, M. Div.

The term 'pericope' is used by New Testament scholars to reference the separate individual stories recorded in the Gospel writings. But they cannot be defined by our traditional term 'story' which has an aspersion of fiction. The pericope must be understood as historical which makes them 'living' encounters in the life and ministry of Jesus. One of the most vital chapters in New Testament, for me, is the 3rd chapter of Mark's Gospel, which I used for sermonic discourse at St. James AME Church for Mother's Day this month. Several pericope are combined in this chapter that clearly span an undesignated time period. It is the task of the New Testament Literary Scholar to define the scope of each pericope and make each one available for it's own historical interpretation.

Barbara Woods Riles Washington

The pericope known as **'The Centurion's Servant'** is a double tradition. To introduce Lachmann's and Wellhausen's work in Synoptic Source theories; I say here that in order to understand them while studying New Testament Literature, I wrote by hand the entire Gospel of Mark with a red ink pen. I then wrote by hand Matthew's Gospel skipping spaces and filling in only the verses that duplicated/mirrored Mark in red pen also. I did the same for Luke. This is THE TRIPLE TRADITION. I returned to my hand written copy of Matthew and Luke filling in with black ink the verses that duplicated/mirrored just these two Gospel writers. This is THE DOUBLE TRADITION. I completed this masterpiece using a blue pen for

✝ 10

"The Voice Of A Proud Community"
Nashville P*R*I*D*E
Pulpit, Pew and Public

the SINGLE TRADITION in Matthew and a green pen for the SINGLE TRADITION in Luke. The finished product is 'a work of art!'; a 'masterpiece'— a piece of The Master!.

Matthew's account of the 'Centurion's Servant' places us at the New Testament's first use of both 'logos/word' and 'pistis/faith'. Word AS Faith. Word IS Faith. This revelation is not abstract. It is not common, neither is it ordinary.

First, Jesus saw the humility of the Centurion. While Luke records that the Centurion sent elders to Jesus, (who took liberty to tell Jesus of the Centurion's worthiness— of his love for the national life, of his building of synogogue) Matthew begins with the Centurion's personal encounter with Jesus and both record the Centurion's self evaluation, *"I am not worthy!"*

A man of position and resolve; defender of nation; owner of property to include one (or more) slaves; builder of the house of worship— one can only imagine the substance of his own home. Yet, as a DOUBLE TRADITION, the Centurion goes out to meet Jesus and says, *"I am not worthy for you to come under my roof." "Speak a Word..."* Right here! Right now!

Jesus saw the Centurion's FAITH and Jesus spoke a WORD! ■

An Invitation to Study Bible Thursdays, 6:30 pm
mustardseedfaith@bellsouth.net

May 25, 2007

Faith of a mustard seed
by Barbara Woods-Washington, M. Div.

"Not even in Israel have I seen such faith!" There was something about this centurion— his attitude? His disposition? His spirit, maybe? His outlook? His humility? His heart, maybe? (I have been told on numerous occasions across the years after proclaiming The Word that I had touched their heart! It is so easy for me to tell when 'your heart ain't in it!' I know that it is true— what comes from the heart, reaches the heart!.) Perhaps Jesus saw this centurion's heart? But, something about this centurion places him first in the New Testament's model for faith.

"Not even in Israel...". Jesus boldly compares this centurion's faith to the lineage of such a great nation, and so that no mistake is made here, the founding fathers, the patriarchs are named! What is this faith that Jesus saw in just this small encounter with this centurion that he had not seen *"even in Israel"*?

Key, for me, in this faith event is the fact that so many of the persons of the centurion station's thoughts, words and deeds towards the personhood of Jesus was to destroy him. Jesus had no money. He had no property. He had no concern for or pursuit of food, shelter or clothing! He had no participation in the national life. He built no house(s) of worship! His 'homelessness' was by design! All Jesus had was 'His Word' which as he spoke it to persons of sufferance, they began to follow him around. And yet, he never used the means of those who followed him to alter his 'homeless existence'; which, I think, is a

Barbara Woods Riles Washington

☦ 11

"The Voice Of A Proud Community"
Nashville P*R*I*D*E
Pulpit, Pew and Public

very vital part of the power of 'His Word'! He never took anything from his followers! To be sure, he charged his disciples to *"take nothing..."*

Jesus had already begun to identify in his 'Word' to the disciples that those of the extreme opposite (the centurion kind) would— (and to be sure did) come to take his life.

Enter a centurion who came taking thought for the wellness of his slave. (Suspect in my small modern mind of course, as a descendent of slaves— he needed him well to continue the servitude.) But Jesus saw something else! *"Not even in Israel have I seen such faith!"* ■

*An Invitation to Study Bible
Thursdays. 6:30 pm
mustardseedfaith@bellsouth.net*

June 1, 2007

Faith of a mustard seed
by Barbara Woods-Washington, M. Div.

Young's identifies the second use of the word 'pistis/faith' in the New Testament pericope known as **'The Healing of The Paralytic'**. It is a Triple Tradition and this faith event is the first use of the word 'pistis/faith' by both Mark and Luke. (It is the task of the New Testament Redaction scholar to look at the prominence that Matthew alone places on 'The Centurion's Servant' faith event in his Gospel); but, turning now to "The Healing of The Paralytic"— (Matthew 9:1-8); (Mark 2:1-12) and (Luke 5:17-26). Jesus came home to his own city and, here too, the word had spread of the power of 'his word' for healing.

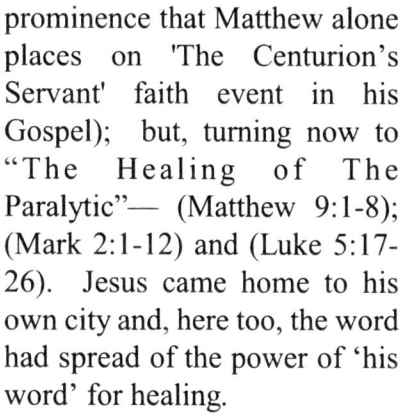

It is no small thing that for the second time New Testament faith begins with the belief that Jesus can heal. Faith is healing. Healing is faith.

Barbara Woods Riles Washington

I am reminded of my responsibilities for the Sick and Shut-in Ministry at both Salem (Harlem) and Central (Atlanta) which at both churches, this task came with the position of Associate to the Pastor. Coming to terms with the fact that sickness— in all of it's varying degrees and forms, (not bound by gender, race, economics, age) —knows no discrimination! Sickness, I suspect, is the most humbling experience of a life. The most cheerful life; the most prideful and arrogant; the atheist, the wealthiest; the most disinherited life— all experience a transition in both personality and character when affliction comes.

To be sure, many of the world's greatest men and women of faith recant their faith journey's beginning, renewal or

"The Voice Of A Proud Community"
Nashville P*R*I*D*E
Pulpit, Pew and Public

'new life' ('born again-ness') at a point when healing came. The more deadly the disease the more praise worthy the healing.

It is clear that Jesus is looking at (your/my) faith! The Centurion came to Jesus seeking healing for his servant and Jesus saw his faith. Now, those close to the paralytic bring him to Jesus for healing, and he saw their faith.

Sickness is not just the physical condition, but is also psychological in diagnosis. I can't help but continue to recognize the "3/5th of a person" law which was legislated upon the African in slavery in America. The result of which is not lost upon the descendants. Many personality disorders that require 'knowing they exist' in order to 'seek healing'. The anger, the violence that erupts so readily in our times leads me to see clearly how and why New Testament faith begins with the belief that Jesus can heal.

Healing is spiritual. Sin sickness! "There's a stranger in the city, He's healing!". I heard them sing it— "I just got the news this morning, healing! A stranger in the city, healing. He's healing the body, Jesus is healing, the sin sick soul." ∎

An Invitation to Study Bible
Thursdays, 6:30 pm
mustardseedfaith@bellsouth.net

June 8, 2007

Faith of a mustard seed
by Barbara Woods-Washington, M. Div.

Present at **'The Healing of The Paralytic'** faith event were Scribes, the office of which plays a major role in the teaching ministry of Jesus. To be sure, many of the most radical sayings that place Jesus in direct conflict with those things that were established in both the religious and national life were pronounced as a direct result of the probing and questioning of the Scribes. Such is the case on this occasion.

The person and position of the Scribe has already been made clear by Jesus in his 'Sermon On The Mount' where he tells 'the following' and ever growing multitude that *"unless your righteousness exceeds the righteousness of the scribe... you cannot enter the Kingdom of Heaven."*

When I was studying Old Testament Literature, I came upon a picture of an ancient Egyptian Scribe. The discussion centered around his life's commitment to the transmission of faith. His papyrus was hand made using the reed plant from the Nile; the finished scrolls of which are still being view today. One of our professors asked the class what direction we would take in ministry? I replied, "I want to be a scribe!"

Barbara Woods Riles Washington

Ezra was a scrivener, *"skilled in the Laws of Moses"*, whose responsibility for the transmission of faith came at a time of exile. His people were displaced, disenfranchised, disinherited— (among other 'dises'), when the King wrote that *"Ezra had the wisdom of (his) God in his hand..."*

It must be borne in mind that there is no 'written word' for Jesus to 'rise and read in the synagogue' in his 'bar mitzvah' days— without the scribe.

The Voice Of A Proud Community
Nashville P*R*I*D*E
Pulpit, Pew and Public

✝ 13

Most conscious, then, of the presence of the scribes, Jesus' pronouncement to the Paralytic takes a radical turn as all three Gospel writer's record him saying, *"your sins are forgiven!"* In the midst of a healing faith ministry, Jesus takes the opportunity (with scribes present) to deliver a direct 'word of forgiveness of sin' which had previously been the sole ownership of God in the priesthood. So as not to mistake the weightiness of the matter, the scribe's response was *"blasphemy!"*

It is my belief that Jesus is granting a personal permission to remove the guilt and shame traditionally associated with sin from a belief system that enabled the oppressive forces of evil to hold sway over life. I think that this systematic oppression, as it relates to authoritative 'sin forgiving power' is, and in itself a vital part of disease. No need to wait for the order to come from the 'holiest of holy', you are free NOW to disassociate sin from disease. Let the healing begin... ∎

An Invitation to Study Bible
Thursdays. 6:30 pm
mustardseedfaith@bellsouth.net

_____
June 15, 2007
_____

Faith of a mustard seed
by Barbara Woods-Washington, M. Div.

"Which is easier to say *'your sins are forgiven'* or to say *'rise and walk'?"* (Matt 9:5) (Mark 2:9) (Luke 5:23). This question that Jesus raises in **'The Healing of the Paralytic'** faith event remains a mystery to many biblical scholars who have written commentaries on scripture. What is clear to most is Jesus' issue, here, with authority: *"so that you will know that the Son of Man has authority on earth to forgive sins..."*

Having already given his attention, first, to 'The Paralytic', saying directly to him *"your sins are forgiven"*, Jesus now turns his attention to the scribes (and Pharisees in Luke) addressing them purely on the basis of their thinking. They didn't have to say much, Jesus already knew what they were thinking and he said, *"why do you question thus..."* ('think evil' in Matthew) not just in your mind but, he said, *"... in your heart!"*

Barbara Woods Riles Washington

I am reminded of the fact that my mother had triple by-pass in 1971 and quadruple by-pass in 1991. In coming to terms with disease of the heart, it is clear to me why faith places such great demands upon the heart. To be sure, the first, 'and greatest commandment' as Jesus recounted, is loving the Lord with all your/my heart. Such a small organ to have the responsibility for being the 'center of life'. It not only has to house the blood system, but also the belief system!

Jesus directs this question to the 'faith keepers' whose 'minds he blew' away and went straight for their hearts. *"Why do you think evil in your heart?"* Easier? I contend that both

☦ 14

"The Voice Of A Proud Community"
Nashville P*R*I*D*E
Pulpit, Pew and Public

sayings presented major difficulties for the scribes.

Jesus was so good at seeing 'faith' in persons who came themselves or brought loved ones to him for healing. He was equally as good at seeing the 'doubt' which prevent healing (on whatever level) from taking place. The 'traditional faith' that the scribes were committed to in transmission had no room for the dynamics of the personhood of Jesus. Saying 'your sins are forgiven' was never an option for them. Inconceivable!

It is no small thing that the scribes had begun to follow Jesus around participating in the significance of the phenomenon of the 'Healing Teacher'. In all that they had seen, it was expected to hear Jesus say *"rise and walk"*. Easy for Jesus, yes! Extremely difficult for the scribes. Jesus had now exposed a hole in the faith of the scribes— there was no power to heal!■

An Invitation to Study Bible Thursdays. 6:30 pm mustardseedfaith@bellsouth.net

June 22, 2007

Faith of a mustard seed
by Barbara Woods-Washington, M. Div.

"...he said to the paralytic 'Rise, take up your pallet and go home'." (Matt 9:6) (Mark 2:10-11) Luke 5:24). Jesus' final word in **'The Healing Of The Paralytic'** faith event returns his attention to the Paralytic to speak directly to him, *"Rise..."*

There are no less than eight different New Testament words that all translate into the one English word, 'rise'. Not a small thing at all that God would break into history and send His Son into a Greek speaking world. The thought taken for the language alone persuades me of this choice.

The word for rise here is 'egeiro' and takes me again to 'my life's word' (John 5) as stated earlier. Jesus says the exact same thing to the triple tradition paralytic that he says to the man sitting 38 years at Bethzatha, *"Rise, take up your pallet...."* I have preached the John 5 text on numerous occasions across the years using the subject 'Rise In The Imperative'.

Having recognized that our translation(s) of scripture say 'rise' in the place of so many different words, it is easy to see why confusion reigns. I am reminded of the word love as a single English translation for no less than three different words in the original language of scripture. I am convinced that this contributes to the mass hysteria in our times when it comes to matters of love— (of God; of man; etc) on all it's levels.

Rise, then for this purpose, must be looked at in reference to just the usage of, 'egeiro'. Where the English verb is very limited in 'mood', the Greek verb accommodates the mood of

Barbara Woods Riles Washington

✝ 15

"The Voice Of A Proud Community"
Nashville P*R*I*D*E
Pulpit, Pew and Public

the speaker. In all four Gospels' reference here, 'egeiro/rise' is in the Greek imperative—'mood of command'. This imperative mood is so misunderstood in the English language that it is defined as being used to tell someone to do something without argument. It's usage is most often defined within the scope of parental authority.

In both Classical and New Testament Greek, the imperative mood is reserved for use only by persons of authority with most all references to use by gods, kings and commanders of armies. Commands that are given in the imperative mood must be carried out as though life depended upon it.

The tense of this verb usage has also given problems to the English grammarians in that here, 'egeiro/rise' is in the 'aorist tense', (not found in English). For the Greek, the aorist tense is not a simple past, present or future action but one that is 'perfect' and used only by god(s)! In the 'Healing of the Paralytic' faith event, 'rise' is in the aorist imperative!

What am I saying? That Jesus' use of the word 'egeiro/rise' in the 'Healing of The Paralytic' faith event is a perfect command that can only be given by God. The hearer must carry out the command as though his life depends upon it. When used by God it has the meaning of 'to awaken from sleep'; 'to rise from the dead'. Where it appears that there was 'no life', 'no health', 'no consciousness', we receive a word from Jesus that says— you must get up, you have to get up; you have life, you have health, you have consciousness. I have made all provisions for you to GET UP! It is IMPERATIVE that you RISE!■

An Invitation to Study Bible Thursdays, 6:30 pm mustardseedfaith@bellsouth.net

---

June 29, 2007

Faith of a mustard seed
by Barbara Woods-Washington, M. Div.

Young's third New Testament occurrence of the word 'pistis/faith' is another triple tradition pericope known simply as **'A Woman's Faith'** which sits in the center of 'Jairus' Daughter'. In the simplest of the three accounts, Matthew reports a very brief encounter that this anonymous woman (whose blood had been hemorrhaging for twelve years) has with Jesus as she sought healing (Matthew 9:20-22). And so, for the third time in it's usage, faith is directly related to healing!

Unnamed—just 'a woman', who came up behind Jesus saying *"If I only touch his cloak, I will be made well"*. Jesus turned to her and said, *"take heart..."* (Again with the heart??) How does one "take heart?"

Here the word rendered 'take heart' is 'tharsao' which says many things in reaching a definitive understanding of the summons by Jesus given to this woman for healing. While various translations of scripture read 'take courage'; 'be of good cheer'; other uses of the word gives the sense of 'to dare'; 'to be confident'; 'to be bold'; 'to not be afraid'.

The doors of Salem Church were open during the week as late as 1:00 am. Most Wednesdays after having given leadership to the Bible Study Group followed by the Prayer Meeting Mid-Week Service and housing probably the largest Alcoholic Anonymous Meeting in Harlem, I would leave the Church very late having fulfilled my last duty of the night in locking down and securing the

Barbara Woods Riles Washington

"The Voice Of A Proud Community"
Nashville P*R*I*D*E
Pulpit, Pew and Public

building. My 1969 Cougar (in 1986) was immobile almost as often as it was mobile, so it was common place for me to walk six blocks to the Subway to take the train home to the parsonage. That late at night you hear clearly all footsteps that come up behind you in the streets of New York City. I remember on several occasions stopping and turning around to meet the footsteps face to face as they passed me by. I had to convince several concerned Church officers and members that "I refuse to fear my people!" Even through their protests, I walked the streets coming to terms with what it means to have a conscious readiness and preparedness to do ministry at any and all times. This with a confidence, a boldness— daring to be available to The Presence of what developed my sense that 'God is with me!'. No— never alone!

This woman, not significant enough to be named in the history of Bible, knew that for twelve years in this condition *"no one could help her"* (Luke 8:43-48). Even after spending all that she had as she continuously sought out physicians, she only grew worse (Mark 5:25-34). So small is her encounter with Jesus that it is recorded as an interruption, an interference, an intrusion in Jesus' mission to 'go and see' about Jairus' daughter. Yet important enough to release a summons from Jesus in the midst of her disease that speaks across the pages of time. Courageous enough, bold enough, daring enough to walk up on Jesus, yet faint-hearted at the point of meeting him face to face. As in the previous two faith events, here and still again, Jesus sees faith. *"Don't loose heart now"*, He said to her, *"your faith has made you well!"* ■

An Invitation to Study Bible Thursdays. 6:30 pm
mustardseedfaith@bellsouth.net

_____
July 6, 2007
_____

Faith of a mustard seed
by Barbara Woods-Washington, M. Div.

The discipline with which it has taken to write this column at times became, to say the least, overwhelming. Looking now I can see where I passed over the Fourth occurrence of 'pistis/faith' in Matthew's Gospel known as **'Two Blind Men Healed'**. As ususal, God has a plan for time and space and now, in 2013, I digress.

Returning now to write concerning this 'Single Tradition' Faith Event. Things are now moving so swiftly in the Healing Faith ministry of Jesus that in this 9th Chapter Jesus is following Jairus home to see about his deceased daughter in verse 19 when in the very next verse the Woman touched the hem of his garment. By verse 25 he is leaving Jairus' home after having resurrected his daughter. What immediately follows is: *"And as Jesus passed on from there, two blind men followed him, crying aloud, "Have mercy on us, Son of David." When he entered the house, the blind men came to him; and Jesus said to them, "Do you believe that I am able to do this?" They said to him, "Yes, Lord." Then he touched their eyes, saying, "According to your faith be it done to you." And their eyes were opened. And Jesus sternly charged them, "See that no one knows it." But they went away and spread his fame through all that district".*

Did you ever wonder where the so very simple, and so awesomely powerful refrain comes from that is a cornerstone of the Church of God In Christ? It is the response that the two Blind Men gave to Jesus' question "Do you believe that I am able to do this?" They said *"YES"*. Yes. Yes. Yes. Yes. Can't you hear them— Yes Lord. Yes Lord, Yes. Yes Lord. The ultimate affirmation of faith that does not even appear in the consciousness of other denominations.

Since man has historically and universally determined that crying jeopardizes manhood, it is sinful to have not come into

"The Voice Of A Proud Community"
Nashville P*R*I*D*E
Pulpit, Pew and Public

the biblical meaning of 'krazontes'— 'crying aloud'. This term has the meaning of 'to croak or cry with a loud and raucous voice'; 'a war cry'; 'to demand with cries'; 'to lament'. In the Old Testament it is dominant in the Psalms and the Prophets where this crying aloud is to God in times of individual and national emergency. Proof of Life in the midst of death and destruction; the crying aloud, the moan, the groan— the wailing. But always, always to God who alone can deliver from the throes of sin and evil. In the New Testament Paul's use of 'krazontes' is very rare, but best stated in the Romans 8 discourse: "We know that the whole creation has been groaning in travail... inwardly...". Jesus cried aloud, "Abba..," in the midst of his ultimate crisis.

As the year 2013 comes to an end I have experienced the Lincoln Monument as a "Wailing Wall" in America. After attending the Saturday, August 24th March on Washington and hearing a segment of Americans lay the issues of this people at the feet of Abraham Lincoln, just 4 days later a separate segment representing the same people again laid the issues at Lincoln's feet. But it has not stopped there. While The United States Congress sought to show their 'godless' powers in shutting down the heartbeat, the legs and hands and feet continue week after week as more and more segments of Americans move to lay their burdens at the feet of Mr. Lincoln.

These two blind men followed Jesus crying aloud— "Have mercy on us, Son of David." Jesus said to them "Do you believe that I am able to do this?" They gave the most important response in all of the history of religion— They said "Yes Lord. Yes. Lord. Yes. Yes. Yes Lord."■

An Invitation to Study Bible Thursdays, 6:30 pm
mustardseedfaith@bellsouth.net

✞ **16B** • *published November 29, 2013*

Faith of a mustard seed
by Barbara Woods-Washington, M. Div.

"O woman, great is your faith!" (Matthew 15:21-28). The fifth use of 'pistis/faith' in New Testament is a double tradition known as **'The Syrophoenician Woman'** (Mark 7:27-30) This woman whose daughter was severely 'demon-possessed', even as a foreigner, had gotten the word of Jesus' power to heal. So little information is given about the details of this faith encounter that even less has been said about it by commentators across the ages.

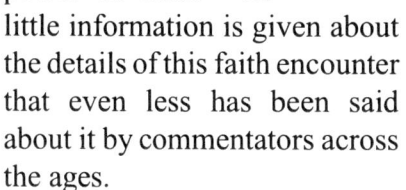

Many have given emphasis to the fact that this woman is a Canaanite and a gentile. Clearly it is a problem for Jesus as well as the disciples, specifically as Matthew's account says Jesus' first response to her was to ignore her cry for mercy— *"not a word did he answer"*. It is the disciples who speak on it suggesting that Jesus *"send her away"*. When Jesus does speak, he clarifies his mission to the disciples by saying *"I was not sent, except to the Lost Sheep of Israel."*

Again, an intrusion in his mission. Now by a woman whose confidence in his ability to help her in the healing of her daughter knows no shame. Having already addressed him with the messianic title— *"O Lord, Son of David"*, she presses on through this very unusual mood for Jesus (yet typical for the disciples). This woman goes up to Jesus and 'throws herself prostrate before him' (the word is 'prosekunei/worshipped') with her continued cry for mercy.

What all Jesus saw in this woman who 'was not of the house of Israel' can only be left to the 'mind's eye' as many a

Barbara Woods Riles Washington

✝ 17

"The Voice Of A Proud Community"
Nashville P*R*I*D*E
Pulpit, Pew and Public

great preacher has told. Whatever he saw, he said to her *"it is not good to take the children's bread and throw it to the dogs!"*

With so many children in my very northern city childhood home, I am mindful even today of my mama's rule on dogs lain down on an occasion when one of my brothers brought home a dog he had found: "if it cannot walk in on two feet, it has no place in my house!" With so many mouths to feed there was no food to throw to the dogs.

But this woman, again an interruption in the mission of Jesus, 'took heart' in responding to Jesus by saying, *"Yes Lord, yet even the dogs eat the crumbs that fall from their master's table."*

I get this woman's confidence, I get her humility, her trust, her reverence, her perseverance, compassion, determination, her 'hutzpah'— an unmitigated boldness that gave her to respond to Jesus the way she did. Whatever Jesus saw in her he said, *"O woman, great is your faith!"* ■

An Invitation to Study Bible Thursdays. 6:30 pm mustardseedfaith@bellsouth.net

---

July 13, 2007

Faith of a mustard seed
by Barbara Woods-Washington, M. Div.

"O faithless and perverse generation, how long am I to be with you? How long am I to bear with you?" (Matt 17:17). This pericope known as **'The Epileptic Boy Healed'** is next in 'pistis/faith' occurrences in New Testament and is designated another triple tradition. Where Matthew and Luke mirror each other in the telling of this faith event, (Luke 9:40-43), Mark has a more detailed account (Mark 9:18-28).

Look first at the word that Jesus uses to directly describe the generation— 'diestrammene/perverse' (diastre). A clear English translation of this word, (used by most all versions of Bible), perverse is defined by Webster as 'turned the wrong way'; 'deviating from the right'; 'obstinate and willful in the wrong'. A quick look at it's usage in Greek, references Aristotle's Ethics— "deficiency in inner attitude leads to confusion and illusion regarding the starting point of action". And in Stoic ethics— "moral corruption of the empirical man... by bad teaching and example and by environmental influences of all kinds".

Barbara Woods Riles Washington

It must be borne in mind that Jesus is speaking to his disciples in this very timely estimation of personhood. How easy it is to place such a callous diagnosis upon those outside the house of faith, but— Jesus is talking about the disciples.

While it is my purpose in this column to promote a 'new thought', I recognize that it's the same 'old story'. So many life encounters are conjured up by this word 'perverse' as Jesus speaks to us. To begin with,

"The Voice Of A Proud Community"
Nashville P*R*I*D*E
Pulpit, Pew and Public

'obstinate and willful in wrong'. The tense and mood of this verb occurrence is reflected upon the act. Leaders and their followers (disciples), both religious and political, perpetuate falsehood so that once the wrong is discovered no attempt is made by the personhood to right the wrong, but takes on a character of obstinance, arrogant, unyielding willfulness in the permanency of the wrong. My grandmother said that you have to "live a lie!". But not just the individual— Jesus is speaking of an entire generation. It becomes a way of life.

The late notorious Dr. Isaac R. Clark, who spent his life in Homiletic Education, taught preachers to preach about "the stink in their nose." The fact that children in our very own households are being molested at earlier and earlier ages 'stinks in my nose'. What has become a very perverse way of life for the generations remains the 'best kept secret in the house'— of faith.

It is a tampering with the individual's value system which becomes the point of deficiency in the inner attitude that breeds confusion and illusion in actions. Moral corruption, bad teaching, bad example, environmental influences— *"O faithless and perverse generation, how long ...?"* ■

An Invitation to Study Bible Thursdays, 6:30 pm mustardseedfaith@bellsouth.net

---
July 20, 2007

Faith of a mustard seed
by Barbara Woods-Washington, M. Div.

"And Jesus rebuked the demon, and it came out of him, and the boy was cured instantly."

The 'watershed' is a term used to identify that 'turning point' in a life when something happens to change the direction of life. New Testament scholars have strongly discussed 'Peter's Confession' as 'The Watershed' in the life of Jesus. Particularly seen in Mark's account. (Mark 8:27-33). Jesus rebuked the disciples (8:30) and then again in another tense of 'epitimao/rebuke', we hear Peter's rebuke. (8:33).

Returning to **'The Epileptic Boy Healed'** faith event where lies a reoccurrence of Jesus' rebuke. (Matthew 17:14-21). While most all versions agree on 'rebuke' in translation; Webster uses rebuke, reproach and reprove to all define each other.

Barbara Woods Riles Washington

Biblical usage of the tense of 'epitimao/rebuke' is most always used by (hu)man. Then, at best, with limited capabilities. According to Jewish tradition, only to selected individuals is authority given to utter an effective word of rebuke. A clear priority for Jesus in 'the calling' of his disciples for *"he gave them the authority over unclean spirits"*.

In the human use of rebuke there is the sense of threat, blame, punishment and even superiority— but not without a response from Jesus. The disciples rebuked the families who brought their children to Jesus. Jesus responds to the disciples saying *"do not hinder them."* The crowd rebuked blind Bartemaeus threatening him to stay away. Jesus responds that they should allow

✝ 19

"The Voice Of A Proud Community"
Nashville P*R*I*D*E
Pulpit, Pew and Public

him to come. Peter rebuked Jesus at a crucial point in his life and ministry. Jesus spoke to Peter as one possessed by a demon, warning him that he was not on the side of God! Stauffer suggests the only occasion when Jesus allowed human rebuke to go unchecked was on the cross. One of the thieves rebuked the other thief for mocking Jesus; then turned to Jesus and asked 'remember me'. Jesus said to the thief, *"this day you will be with me in Paradise."*

Jesus uses the tense of 'epetimnsen/rebuke' that is most always used by god(s). With a long Old Testament history of God's use of 'rebuke', in New Testament they are rare.

A closer look at the difference between the two biblical tense uses of 'rebuke' suggests that when this Word comes from God it evokes the 'works of God'. Did I forget to mention that Jesus rebuked the wind and rain causing people to say what manner of man is this, that even nature, the elements— goes to work, (or stills) when His Word comes forth.

Jesus is here with this child who has been diagnosed as epileptic. His father, exhausted of his resources for his son's healing brings him to Jesus. Jesus diagnosed 'demoniac'. For this child's healing, *". . . Jesus rebuked the demon, and it came out of him, and the boy was cured instantly."* ■

An Invitation to Study Bible
Thursdays, 6:30 pm
mustardseedfaith@bellsouth.net

July 27, 2007

Faith of a mustard seed
by Barbara Woods-Washington, M. Div.

"And I brought him to your disciples and they could not heal him." Another look at **'The Epileptic Boy Healed'** faith event (Matthew 17:14-21) (Mark 9:14-29) and (Luke 9:37-43).

At what point does a childhood disease that the family— most likely at the diagnosis of a physician is treating as epilepsy, equate with demon possession?? The symptoms were real: He falls into the fire! He falls into the water! Though it is not within the Physicians realm 'to see' an 'unclean spirit', Jesus calls this one 'deaf and dumb'.

Jesus calls, is teaching and preparing the disciples not only 'to see' but to take authority over 'unclean spirits'. So among the other 'misunderstood acts' of Jesus on the part of the disciples, add 'the rebuke command'— their authority over 'unclean spirits'. For the father said to Jesus, *"I brought him (my son) to your disciples and they could not heal him."*

It occurs to me that the limited capabilities that we as humans have in the use of the 'rebuke command' is directly related to motive. Double-mindedness, hidden agendas and the like have rendered the modern disciple of Jesus great personal gain at the expense of a 'demon controlled' church. *"Why could we not cast it out?"* The 'unclean heart' cannot affect an 'unclean spirit'.

Much talk about how many Christians who worship with a high level of commitment, leave the church Sunday after Sunday without ever having experienced any 'God given attention' to our diseases. So many church folks suffering with diseases that go unseen and unknown because it

Barbara Woods Riles Washington

☦ 20

"The Voice Of A Proud Community"
Nashville P*R*I*D*E
Pulpit, Pew and Public

is only Jesus who can 'see and heal' our 'deafness and dumbness'! The disciples just didn't get it.

Christians go from Church to Church, seeking, looking for healing from our diseases and infirmities, turning over our resources to 'disciples' who gain wealth and lay up treasures on earth, but just 'don't get it!' *"Why could we not cast it out?"*

It is no small thing that in each of the faith events that we have look at, there is this urgency to 'get to Jesus'. Whether the disease was physical, spiritual, mental, social; whether it was for personal healing or on the behalf of a loved one— the 'singleness of mind' gave rise to a 'by-passing' of all who were 'in the way' of 'getting to Jesus'. The Centurion had this 'mind set', as did the Paralytic's loved ones. This mind existed in the woman who had been hemorrhaging as well as in the Syrophoenician woman who sought healing for her daughter. The Epileptic boy's father had this mind— 'if I can just get to Jesus...'■

An Invitation to Study Bible Thursdays. 6:30 pm mustardseedfaith@bellsouth.net

August 3, 2007

Faith of a mustard seed
by Barbara Woods-Washington, M. Div.

"...because of your little faith. For truly I tell you, if you have faith the size of a mustard seed, you will say to this mountain, move..." (Matthew 17:20).

The 'Epileptic Boy Healed' faith event is followed by a private moment with the disciples. They were expected to have healing power and this boy's father reported to Jesus that he would not have had to 'get to him' except for the faith failure of his disciples. This consciousness caused the disciples concern for their inability to 'exorcize' authority over demons and they take this opportunity of privacy to ask Jesus, *"why could we not cast it out?"* 'Oligo pistian' = 'little faith'. Spiritual healing powerlessness directly related to 'little faith'.

Jesus used one of the 'littlest seeds' to teach his disciples about the measure of faith. Your faith is little— look at this little seed!

There is no usage of 'mustard seed' in the Old Testament. Biblically, it is found only 5 times— all 5 uses exclusive to Jesus. The 5 becomes 2 as this teaching to measure faith by the 'mustard seed' is a double tradition (Matthew 17:20) and (Luke 17:6); a follow-up to the triple tradition **'The Parable of The Mustard Seed'** (Matthew 13:31-32) (Mark 4:33-32) and (Luke 13:18-19). Jesus has introduced this scripturally new idea that *"the Kingdom of Heaven is like a grain of mustard seed... It is the smallest of all seeds, but when it has grown it is the greatest of shrubs and becomes a tree..."*

I answered a call to ministry while working at Grady Hospital

Barbara Woods Riles Washington

☦ 21

The Voice Of A Proud Community
Nashville P*R*I*D*E
Pulpit, Pew and Public

in Atlanta. I went first as a temp to work in the position of secretary to the Chaplain while Kay was out on Jury Duty. It was my total 're-birth' of religious consciousness since having left home for college seven years earlier. One week in the Hospital Chaplaincy department opened the 'flood gates' accessing all of the 'training up of this child in the ways...'. I went the next week to Personnel D (in the basement of the hospital) then on to some personal organizational projects after the Director of Personnel B, Glen Blackston, took note of my work. Got to work one day and returned to the Chapel and fell on my knees at the alter. Returned one year later to climb the stairs to mount the lectern to preach in the Goddard Memorial Chapel of Grady Memorial Hospital.

There can be no doubt that Jesus is introducing the possibilities of faith. Lay aside the birth genealogies that place him in the line of the Davidic House— scripture would suggest a very humble origin. Manger born in a stable to the house of a carpenter— to one who is sought out by multitudes confident in his power to heal; all based upon a relationship with God whom he knew as his father. If you think, if you believe, if you trust, if you have faith the size of a mustard seed... you can say to a mountain... or to a tree..." ■

An Invitation to Study Bible Thursdays. 6:30 pm mustardseedfaith@bellsouth.net

August 10, 2007

Faith of a mustard seed
by Barbara Woods-Washington, M. Div.

"May no fruit ever come from you again." (Matt 21:19). Next in the 'pistis/faith' occurrences is **'The Cursing Of The Fig Tree'**, a double tradition where Matthew (21:18-22) and Mark (11:12-26) report and Luke is silent. In this faith event no one has approached Jesus for healing.

The fig tree's importance in biblical history is no small affair. Present in the Garden of Eden, this tree is mentioned by name in it's provision of 'material' for the 'first clothing'. When the knowledge of good and evil came and nakedness was realized, Adam and Eve made for themselves 'aprons of fig leaves'. Known throughout Old Testament times as one of the most important fruits in the region, this tree is often referenced in conjunction with the vine. A wealth of materials exist on the medicinal uses of the fig (as in II Kings 20:7 and Isaiah 38:21) where a cake of pressed figs' is used as a 'plaster for healing'. Note must be taken of this tree's unusual ability to bear fruit twice in a year— 'early figs' and 'late figs'. By New Testament times, this tree is a most common part of the scenery and is referenced metaphorically by the greatest of teachers. Amazed, the disciples asked *"how did the fig tree wither at once?" "Faith!"* Jesus says.

While the interpretation of this pericope varies widely, (specifically because many scholars see a textual problem— fruit on the fig tree at Passover season?...), it is clear to me that 'pistis/faith', as we have followed the occurrences of it's word usage in New Testament, is for Jesus, dynamic in scope.

Barbara Woods Riles Washington

☦ 22

"The Voice Of A Proud Community"
Nashville P*R*I*D*E
Pulpit, Pew and Public

I am persuaded by Bornkamm's **'Jesus of Nazareth'** where in his section subtitled 'Faith and Prayer' he writes, "In the tradition of Jesus' sayings faith is always linked with power and miracles." Hunzinger suggests that this faith event stands alone as a 'miracle of judgement' in the Gospels. Others take the metaphorical ground and view the curse as symbolic of 'unfruitful Israel'.

I am mindful of the fact that Jesus is experiencing 'The Passion' having just made his 'Triumphant Entry' into Jerusalem riding on a donkey and 'weeping' over a people who 'would today know the things that make for peace!' That even in the face of his imminent death he is again taking the teaching position for the benefit of his disciples.

Among the many human emotions in the life of Jesus at this moment, he is hungry. He sees a fig tree and approaching it realizes that the tree has no fruit. The 'fully man' side places Jesus in the center of human nature. He curses the tree! He is hungry. The tree's fruit should satisfy the hunger, but it has no fruit. What good is a fig tree with no figs to a hungry man?? He curses the tree! If you cannot feed me when I'm hungry, you will never feed again. He curses the tree while those standing by watch it wither—immediately! *"May no fruit ever come from you again."* ■

*An Invitation to Study Bible Thursdays. 6:30 pm
mustardseedfaith@bellsouth.net*

August 17, 2007

Faith of a mustard seed
by Barbara Woods-Washington, M. Div.

In 1981, when I began serving as Pastor to the Gordon Road United Methodist Church in Atlanta, there was a monthly meeting and annual event of **'Note Singers'**. Every month the local group would gather at 3:00 pm on Sunday afternoon to sing notes. What a time! Then in July, Gordon Road hosted a 'Note Singers Convention' and other groups of Note Singers came for an annual event. They gave me a set of hymn books of notes, but, needless to say— 'Note Singing' is a dying art. I so long to film this culture before it's extinction. I did, however, discover that I could sing verse for verse many of the old hymns, many of which I had not heard sung in my adult life. As the words came forth it caused me to wonder where they were coming from.

By the time I got to Salem in 1985, I would sometimes look up and see that persons were watching me sing hymns as they began to notice that I very rarely opened the hymnal for singing. It was not until my mother's passing in 2002 when I became heir to my family's pictorial collection that I discovered a wonderful picture dated in the 1940's. It is an 8x10 of the pulpit view of my birth church, the Cedar Avenue Church of God in Cleveland, Ohio. Pictured in the Choir are my grandmother, Ruth Magby Smith and my great-grandmother, Rosa Marshall Magby Cross. It has now dawned on me that I was born in the choir.

The hymns of faith have been a very important part of the Black Church's tradition and Black American culture at large. Both Howard Thurman and

Barbara Woods Riles Washington

☦ 23

"The Voice Of A Proud Community"
Nashville P*R*I*D*E
Pulpit, Pew and Public

James Cone have put into theological perspective this phenomenon of song as a vital part of our faith history as a people. In *'Deep River'* (1945) and *'The Negro Spiritual Speaks of Life and Death'* (1947) Howard Thurman makes this statement: "My own life has been so deeply influenced by the genius of the spirituals that the meaning as distilled into my experience in my early years spills over in much that I have come to think in my maturity."

In *'The Spirituals and The Blues'* (1972) James Cone writes: "Existentially, the subject matter and focus of this book have been defined by the black musical forms which have influenced my life. I have written about the spirituals and the blues because I have lived the experience which created them... I affirmed the reality of the spirituals and blues as authentic expressions of my humanity, responding to the rhythms of dance. I, therefore, write about the spirituals and blues, because I am the blues and my life is a spiritual. Without them, I cannot be."

By the time this column is published, I will be in Atlanta to participate in the Ebony Black Family Reunion Tour 2007. In preparation for this, I have thought so much this week about the words of this hymn— "Faith of our mothers! Living still. In spite of dungeon, fire, and sword. O How our hearts beat high with joy. Whene'er we hear that glorious word! Faith of our mothers, holy faith! We will be true to thee til death."■

An Invitation to Study Bible Thursdays. 6:30 pm
mustardseedfaith@bellsouth.net

August 24, 2007

Faith of a mustard seed
by Barbara Woods-Washington, M. Div.

"Woe to you, scribes and Pharisees, hypocrites! For you tithe mint, dill, and cummin, and have neglected the weightier matters of the law: justice and mercy and faith." (Matt 23:23). As a 'last will and testament' of Jesus, Matthew's final usage of 'pistis/faith' is a double tradition pericope known as **'The Woes Against The Pharisees'** (Matt 23:1-36) and (Luke 11:39ff)

I am hard pressed to enter this text first with the 'justice theme'. Not simply because it is first in the order of the 'weightier matters of the law', but more so because it has resounded in my consciousness so lately as I experience the Justice system in our times— 'no justice, no peace!'

Judaism, the religion of Jesus, is a legalistic based faith. Clearly, a definitive 'new beginning' of this major world religion can be seen in the personhood of Moses, 'The Law Giver'. This people's 'covenant' with God gave them a theocratic government where God is ruler, judge and king— even through the coming of Jesus whose life times were in an Empire in which 'freedom of religion' was only decreed to them.

It must be borne in mind that the Prophets of Israel, 'the Nabi', is 'the mouthpiece' of God. It is during the most difficult years in the national life of the Old Testament faith— through the wars and two exiles, that God speaks most urgently and consistently through the prophets concerning justice. *"Woe to you, scribes and Pharisees, hypocrites... neglected the weightier matters of the law: justice..."*

The Voice Of A Proud Community
Nashville P*R*I*D*E
Pulpit, Pew and Public

It is no small thing that some thought Jesus to be one of the prophets. Just as all the prophets before him spoke of there being no justice in the land— *"there is lying, stealing and killing"*— Jesus, too, raises a prophetic voice.

All uses of 'krisis/judgement' in Matthew are in the mouth of Jesus. The tense here is 'krisin', rendered justice and/or judgement by most all translations. This tense is used by Jesus only in relationship to the Pharisees, the religious leaders of his faith. First, in Matt 12:14ff, he becomes aware that the Pharisees have held counsel to destroy him and in withdrawing from them he speaks of fulfillment of Isaiah's prophesy— 'The Servant of God', beloved, sent to bring justice/judgement to victory. Now, *"Woe to you, scribes and Pharisees, hypocrites... neglected the weightier matters of the law: justice..."*

Jesus has come down to the end of his life, in the throes of 'The Passion'— and equally as disturbed about the state of the people of God as were all the prophets before him. As a 'last will and testament' he speaks to the religious leaders: *"Woe to you, scribes and Pharisees, hypocrites! For you tithe mint, dill, and cummin, and have neglected the weightier matters of the law: justice..."* ■

*An Invitation to Study Bible
Thursdays, 6:30 pm
mustardseedfaith@bellsouth.net*

August 31, 2007

Faith of a mustard seed
by Barbara Woods-Washington, M. Div.

"Woe to you, scribes and Pharisees, hypocrites! . . . ." (Matt 23:23).

Most prominent among the 'denominations' of Judaism in Jesus' times is the Pharisees. Although Paul has identified himself as a Pharisee, the verdict is still out on Jesus' sect.

When Israel returned from Babylonian exile, there is no attempt made to restore the monarchy. Under the leadership of Ezra— the 'New Law Giver', a 'theocratic rule' is re-established; with responsibilities for guidance given to the high priest. The 'new law'— Leviticus, incorporated 'The Priestly Code', and speaks to a 'new people': *"You shall be holy to me; for I, the Lord am holy, and I have separated you from the other peoples to be mine."* (Leviticus 20:26)

The Pharisees— 'those who are separated' adopted the principles of 'holiness' prescribed to the 'letter of the law'; and regarded themselves the 'heirs to Ezra's teachings'. Their beginnings as a movement date to the Maccabeean times and can be accounted for in the 'Apocryphal/ Deutrocannonical' Books of Scripture— "a company of pious Jews, brave men from Israel, none but those who willingly submitted themselves to the law." (I Maccabees 2:42). 'Separating lines' are subsequently drawn from the Hasmoneans who sought political power. The Pharisees became known for their pious living, prayers and fasting in preparation for the 'Kingdom of God'. Although there were priests among the Pharisees, it was their scribes who held the positions of leadership.

Barbara Woods Riles Washington

"The Voice Of A Proud Community"
Nashville P*R*I*D*E
Pulpit, Pew and Public

† 25

Perhaps it was because of their lack of participation in the political life, that by the time Jesus of Nazareth appears in the Roman Empire, the Pharisees have become a religious force to reckon with— and 'reckon with them' Jesus does. In the presence of the Pharisees, Jesus: sat at dinner with the tax collectors and sinners (Matt 9:10f); allowed his disciples to pluck grain to eat on the Sabbath (Matt 12:1f); allowed his disciples to eat without washing their hands (Matt 15:1f); and upbraided the Pharisees for their hard-heartedness in questions of divorce (Matt 19:3f). In the presence of the Pharisees, Jesus speaks two of the three most important Parables of his ministry, both of which took aim directly at them— the 'Parable On Defilement' (Matt 15:1f) and the 'Parable Of The Vineyard' (Matt:20:1f); both of which led to the intensification of the plot by the Pharisees to take his life.

'Weighty' among the matters of conflict between the Pharisees and Jesus are the 'Purity Laws' and the 'Tithe of The Seeds'. Here, now Jesus approaches the 'Tithe of the Seeds'.■

An Invitation to Study Bible Thursdays, 6:30 pm mustardseedfaith@bellsouth.net

_____

September 7, 2007
_____

Faith of a mustard seed
by Barbara Woods-Washington, M. Div.

"Woe to you, scribes and Pharisees, hypocrites! For you tithe mint, dill, and cummin, ..." (Matt 23:23). Continued attention is given to the final use of pistis/faith in Matthew. 'Woe/ouai' is a form of deep distress and is used to express dismay, misfortune, sorrow, and misery. Jesus is now mournful, grievous over the way the Pharisees have become fixed on **'The Tithe of The Seed'** to the neglect of justice, mercy and faith.

From the Testament of Old, followers of Judaism speak of 'Three Pillars' upon which this faith holds fast: Torah, Tithe and Temple. Although the discussion on the 'Three Pillars' varies to include the destruction of the Temples and along with this the shifting of the leadership from priest to rabbi, these 'pillars' define a very long tradition of a people who understood themselves as 'God's chosen'.

For the occasional Bible reader, canonical references to the Tithe could not begin to define it's meaning as a substantive practice for a faith that has survived the forces of history. Neither can the casual modern day Christian, amid a greed driven religiosity, recognize the community building and life sustaining purposes for setting aside a tenth of what was initially 'first fruits' of harvest; for the express purpose of providing food for the tribe of Levi set aside as priests whose only job it was to maintain the activities of the temple— Torah, worship, rituals, feasts and sacrifices.

It is no small thing that Jesus was born, lived and died a Jew for whom faith and race

Barbara Woods Riles Washington

"The Voice Of A Proud Community"
Nashville P*R*I*D*E
Pulpit, Pew and Public

were bound as a single entity. He had been well learned in the Torah and was astute in the Prophets. He was particularly impressed by the prophet Isaiah whose works he could be heard reading and quoting throughout his public ministry.

There can be no doubt of the consistency of the prophetic voices expressing over and over again God's displeasure with the use of the sacrifices being offered. Isaiah said it early, *"What to me is the multitude of your sacrifices? says the Lord;"* (Isaiah 1:11). Jeremiah cried out 'raise a standard', *"For from the least to the greatest of them, everyone is greedy for unjust gain; and from the prophet to the priest, everyone deals falsely."* (Jeremiah 6:13). Martin Luther King, Jr. in his life giving sacrifice for justice, could be heard quoting Amos throughout his public ministry, *"Even though you offer me your burnt offerings and grain offerings, I will not accept them... But let justice roll down like waters, and righteousness like an ever-flowing stream".* (Amos 5:22f).

To show how 'fine print' the Pharisee had become in their obsessive need for the seed tithe, he names those most highly valued for their usage as spices and say, 'what does this have to do with justice, mercy and faith'?■

An Invitation to Study Bible
Thursdays, 6:30 pm
mustardseedfaith@bellsouth.net

September 14, 2007

Faith of a mustard seed
by Barbara Woods-Washington, M. Div.

"Woe to you, scribes and Pharisees, hypocrites! For you tithe mint, dill, and cummin, and have neglected the weightier matters of the law: justice and mercy and faith." (Matt 23:23). The final use of 'pistis/faith' in Matthew is worthy of continuous attention. Just a single verse of scripture out of the mouth of Jesus is so important that it is difficult to pass on by. We have considered the 'justice' theme; The Pharisees; and the 'Tithe of The Seed';— turn now to the weightier matter of mercy.

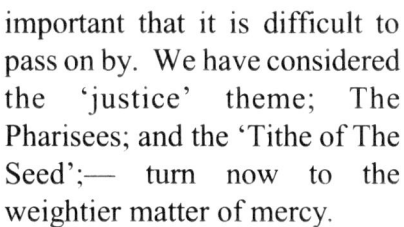

In the Old Testament, 'hesed/mercy', steadfast love is directly related to covenant. Described most often as an emotion or an attitude, mercy arises out of a mutual relationship. It is expected of one from the other. 'Hesed' is what gives security to men in their dealings one to another. It is pledged by one to the other.

The righteous can boast of 'God's hesed'. Mercy, which God has promised, cannot be claimed, but one may certainly expect it. In covenant relationship of trust, and faithfulness, mercy is the appropriate attitude. It is of major concern for God in the voice of the prophets. *"For I desire hesed, and not sacrifice, the knowledge of God rather than burnt offerings."* (Hosea 6:6) I can clearly see the prophetic lineage from Amos to Jesus to Martin in the Micah 6:8 reference: *"He has shown you, O mortal, what is good: and what does the Lord require of you, but to do justice and to love mercy, and to walk humbly with your God."* Still again, the word of the Lord came to Zechariah, saying, *"Thus says*

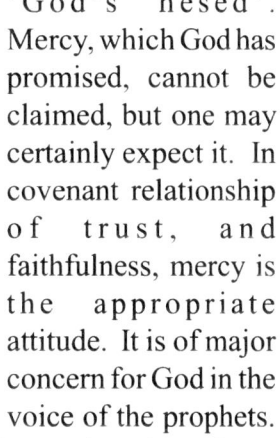

Barbara Woods Riles Washington

the Lord of hosts: render true justice, show kindness and mercy to one another; do not oppress the widow, the orphan, the alien, or the poor; and do not devise evil in your heart against one another." (Zechariah 7:8f).

In the language of later Judaism, mercy and grace are used interchangeably. His mercy is gracious action. He reveals it. It is expected, hoped for, prayed for.

In classical, philosophical Greek, 'eleos/mercy' is the emotion roused by contact with an affliction which comes undeservedly on someone else. Mercy is evoked, specifically, when the other is in trouble. Typical that the emotion of 'eleos' plays a great part in the administration of justice. The accused must seek to arouse the 'eleos' of the judge.

In the New Testament, 'eleos/mercy' is often used for the divinely required attitude of man to man. Kindness which we owe one another in mutual relationships. God's mercy is now thought of as preceding man's. Elsewhere, mercy is concerned for the eternal welfare of others. Howard Thurman talks of the merciful act as an opportunity that you have to 'take advantage' of someone but you chose not to. Jesus in the 'Sermon On The Mount's Beatitudes' says, you are blessed in this choice and that mercy is now promised to you.

I came to know New York City as a place where you must be 'In a New York State Of Mind' in order to survive it's merciless mistreatment of strangers. A part of that 'NY mind' is to be geared against 'theft of person' on a daily basis. Having had four wallets stolen from my purses, I am keenly aware of how personal belongings must be secured. Outside of the city, you can let your purse sit in the shopping cart at the supermarket, walk around with your purse open with items exposed, but the minute you cross a bridge or through a tunnel into The City everything must change in a town where as a way of life, there is no mercy!

As a 'weighter' matter of the law, Jesus is here calling for attention to 'mercy'. ■

*An Invitation to Study Bible
Thursdays. 6:30 pm
mustardseedfaith@bellsouth.net*

September 21, 2007

Faith of a mustard seed
by Barbara Woods-Washington, M. Div.

When I came to Bennett College as Chaplain in July 1988, those students who wanted to sing Gospel music sang in the North Carolina Agricultural and Technical State University Gospel Fellowship Choir. Must take a moment to honor them as the "Muhammad Ali" of College and University Choirs. When their name was said it was never without adding "The Award Winning ...!" And to their Director, Ron Jones who is undisputably #1.

By the spring semester 1989, I instituted Sunday Morning Worship service, first one Sunday monthly, then two. I asked Duncan Butler to form a choir for this service. The choir decided on the name— **"Belles of Harmony Gospel Choir"**.

By the spring semester 1990, a young musician from A&T asked to take over the direction of the choir. Tyrone Stanley in about two weeks prepared the choir, along with new members, for *'Religious Emphasis Week'* in April. I added *'The Gospel Fest'* to the already established activities of the week and The Choir premiered on this occasion.

By faith, the following spring I took the choir on it's first tour. *The 'Campus Ministry '91 Spring Tour'* began with a Friday evening Concert at First COGIC, Brooklyn in new robes. On Saturday morning we started our tour at Battery Park to view the Statue of Liberty. In deciding whether to take the Ferry to the Island, they wanted to see more of the city. We walked to Canal Street where they spent most all of their monies. Across Canal through Washington Square at New York University. The Choir wanted to sing in the Square when they saw the artist's money containers being filled. Out of the Square to West 4th Street in and out of some of my favorite shops. But only God knows the odds of running into a student who had not returned to Bennett that school

Barbara Woods Riles Washington

✝ 28

"The Voice Of A Proud Community"
Nashville P*R*I*D*E
Pulpit, Pew and Public

year. When I heard the screams, my heart raced. Then seeing the surprise on her face made the tour worthwhile.

Caught the A Train to Harlem at West 4th & Broadway. Shortly after getting off the train at 125th Street/MLK, time was running out. I had hoped to get them to The Schomberg at 135th & Lenox/Malcom X where time and place had been given to our Driver. I left them at The Apollo and scurried to get the bus. We arrived, on time, for our Saturday evening Concert at St. Mark's AME, Queens, We worshiped Sunday morning at Hanson Place UMC in Brooklyn and sang a Sunday afternoon Concert at Friendship Baptist, Harlem.

But it didn't stop. After resting a week and accusing Rev. Woods of taking them to New York and trying to kill them, the Choir wanted both a Fall and Spring Tour in the new school year. Requests begun to multiply locally and families were requesting Concerts at home churches. The *'Campus Ministry '91 Fall Tour'* was to Maryland. We did the Friday evening Concert at Antioch Baptist, Upper Marlboro. Our Saturday tour of DC included the Smithsonian with an unforgettable Saturday evening Concert at Interdenominational COGIC, Gaithersburg. I was the Sunday morning preacher with an afternoon Concert at St. John AME, Baltimore. As memorable as this tour was, the day at St. John remains fixed in our hearts.

The *'Campus Ministry '92 Spring Tour'* was a Friday evening second year Concert at First COGIC, Brooklyn. Our Saturday tour included the South Street Pier and on to New Jersey for a Saturday evening Concert at Sharon Baptist, New Brunswick, NJ. I preached the Sunday morning service with an afternoon Concert at Sanctuary Church Of The Open Door, Philadelphia. The day at Sanctuary is still difficult to describe. The Choir talked about Sanctuary Church all the way back to Greensboro, all night, nobody slept. ■

An Invitation to Study Bible Thursdays. 6:30 pm
mustardseedfaith@bellsouth.net

September 28, 2007

Faith of a mustard seed
by Barbara Woods-Washington, M. Div.

"Woe to you, scribes and Pharisees, hypocrites! For you tithe mint, dill, and cummin, and have neglected the weightier matters of the law: justice and mercy and faith." (Matt 23:23). Yet again a look at this final occurrence of faith/pistis in Matthew's Gospel.

Never before have I looked at faith as a 'weightier matter of the law'. And so, in the midst of a new thought, let's follow Matthew in this. When the consideration is given to Jesus' religious context, all discussions surrounding this text places us, again, in the Old Testament— the Law and the Prophets.

To begin with, faith in the Old Testament is man's reaction to God's action— developing a very vital sense of the omnipotence, omniscience and omnipresence of God. In it's oldest traditions, faith is collective. The community experienced the 'acts of God' on their behalf and as 'a people' developed a reaction attitude of both 'fear' and 'trust'. To be sure, the Old Testament history is considered to be a 'salvation history', told from a view of covenant— 'relationship with God'. "If you will be my people, I will be your God!"

For Isaiah, faith and being are one and the same. Weiser has suggested that Isaiah deserves the title as 'The Prophet of Faith'. From the earliest days of his calling, he speaks to kings as though faith is 'the only' state of existence. *"I will wait for the Lord, who is hiding his face from the house of Jacob, and I will hope in him."* (Isaiah 8:17) It is not until The Exile that the 'object of faith' becomes an issue. Convinced that Yahweh/God had forsaken

Barbara Woods Riles Washington

"The Voice Of A Proud Community"
Nashville P*R*I*D*E
Pulpit, Pew and Public

✝ 29

them in the events which led to the destruction of the Temple and the deportations, Israel now sat by the waters of Babylon and wept as they remembered Zion. The Lord's song could not be sung in a strange land.

With Ezra and Nehemiah's restoration of the Temple and Law; the establishment of the Rabbinical tradition; and the canonization of scripture, faith is now 'obedience to the Law'. No longer a relationship where God's acts are seen as 'present' in the history of Israel and their participation, their deeds no longer determined their destiny. Schlatter provokes thought when he writes "Faith loses the character of present decision in the historical situation and thus represents itself as something static and enduring, as the form of consciousness which results from the entrance of scriptural doctrine therein."

Now that the 'object of faith' has become 'The Law', it is no small thing that in summing up 'The Law', Jesus has placed 'The Lord, Our God' back in the very center of life. In this 'woe' over the preoccupation with laws that are of little substance— (not even the TEN, which he reduces to TWO), he says to the Pharisees and scribes, return to the 'law of faith'. ■

*An Invitation to Study Bible
Thursdays, 6:30 pm
mustardseedfaith@bellsouth.net*

October 5, 2007

Faith of a mustard seed
by Barbara Woods-Washington, M. Div.

As a summary of the use of 'faith/pistis' in Matthew's Gospel, Young's Analytical Concordance identified eight (8) uses of this form in Matthew and all eight are found in the mouth of Jesus. It is exclusively 'red letter'— as the popular song goes "He said it, I believe it. I'm gonna take Him at His Word!"

First, Jesus said to those who followed him in response to the centurion: (1) *"Truly I tell you, not even in Israel have I seen such faith!"* Next, when Jesus (2) saw the faith of the friends who were carrying the bed of a paralyzed man to get him to Jesus, he said to the paralytic: *"Take heart, son; your sins are forgiven."*

Then, suddenly, the woman who had been hemorrhaging for twelve years came up and touched his cloak. He said to her: (3) *"Take heart, daughter, your faith has made you well."* Now, two blind men follow him from the leader of the synagogue's (Jairus') house crying loudly "Have mercy on us, Son of David!" Jesus said to them, "Do you believe that I am able to do this?" Their response is THE most important 'affirmation of faith' sung in the Black Church tradition— "YES, LORD!" He touched their eyes and said: (4) *"According to your faith let it be done to you."*

Next, the Canaanite woman who shamelessly sought Jesus in the healing of her daughter. Jesus said to her: (5) *"Woman, Great is your faith! Let it be done for you as you wish."* Then, the father of an epileptic son told Jesus his disciples were unable to cure the boy. Jesus says: "You faithless and perverse generation, how much

Barbara Woods Riles Washington

☦ 30

"The Voice Of A Proud Community"
Nashville P*R*I*D*E
Pulpit, Pew and Public

longer must I be with you? Bring him to me." When the disciples question their lack of power, he says to them: "Because of your little faith. For truly I tell you, (6) *if you have faith the size of a mustard seed, you will say to this mountain, 'move from here to there' and it will move; and nothing will be impossible for you."*

Hunger is upon Jesus and the fig tree in his path has no fruit. Cursing the tree, his disciples question and he says to them: (7) *"Truly I tell you, if you have faith and do not doubt, not only will you do what has been done to the fig tree, but even if you say to this mountain, 'be lifted up and thrown into the sea,' it will be done. Whatever you ask for in prayer with faith, you will receive it."*

Bennett College is one of the last HBCU's with required Chapel attendance— during my chaplaincy known as 'ACES' (Academic and Cultural Enrichment Series), every Tuesday and Thursday at 11:00am. In creatively designing these programs for excellence, I added "The Last Lecture" series and asked Faculty to sum up what they believed to be the most important issues of a particular course of study. The (8)th and final use of faith/pistis by Jesus in Matthew is perhaps his "Last Lecture": *"Woe to you, scribes and Pharisees, hypocrites! For you tithe mint, dill and cummin, and have neglected the weightier matters of the law: justice and mercy and faith. It is these you ought to have practiced without neglecting the others. You blind guides! You strain out a gnat but swallow a camel!"* ∎

An Invitation to Study Bible Thursdays, 6:30 pm
mustardseedfaith@bellsouth.net

October 12, 2007

Faith of a mustard seed
by Barbara Woods-Washington, M. Div.

I learned my freshman year in Seminary, 1978, of three annual events that I could not miss.

First was the Anniversary of the **Atlanta Gospel Movement** at the Grace Covenant Baptist Church. It was gospel music as I had not experienced it. Among their annual guests was the Cathedral of Faith COGIC 'Showers of Blessings Choir'. The first time I heard them sing, this choir had me pinned to my seat. They sang from the prophet Hosea in the tune of Beethoven's 5th Symphony— "If my people, would just humble themselves, humble themselves and turn, from their wicked ways, then will I hear from heaven!"

Then there was Revival at Antioch Baptist Church. Pastor Cameron Alexander's name is to be said in reverence. A very close friend and I would slip away from Central on any Sunday that Dr. Lowery was away from the pulpit and head down Northside Drive to Antioch. But each year of my three Seminary years, I attended all five nights of Caesar Clark's annual Revival at Antioch. He was known as 'the preacher's preacher'. Just can't explain it.

And then there was King Week. During my student ministry years at Central, the Pastor's wife, Evelyn Gibson Lowery founded the Southern Christian Leadership Conference/ WOMEN. As a founding member, I attended her in many of the events that the SCLC/WOMEN planned and sponsored. Her vision for the 'Drum Major Awards Banquet' is one that lives on with greatness. I was a hostess at the first Banquet. Got 'pushed' by

Barbara Woods Riles Washington

"The Voice Of A Proud Community"
Nashville P*R*I*D*E
Pulpit, Pew and Public

☦ 31

Martin Luther King, Senior as I led him to his seat. He had 'shown up' in the doorway of our Homiletics (preaching) class on a day that Professor Mance Jackson was away. At the Banquet, on our way to his table he bumped me (I guess to let me know he remembered me from class) and said to me "so you wanna preach, huh?"

Evelyn had also gotten the organization involved in some very important issues to include the 'Missing and Murdered Children's Crisis' of Atlanta while the city was in the throes of this demonic force. Many of the mothers of these children joined SCLC/WOMEN as Evelyn's vision began to manifest.

SCLC sponsored the First 'King Week' at this time and I participated in most all of the events. Most memorable for me of the activities was the Arts Program held at Wheat Street Baptist Church on Auburn Avenue, a stone's throw from SCLC headquarters. Stephanie Mills sang. But a young white male did the most anointed liturgical dance I have yet to witness. Dressed as a battered soldier of Jewish faith, the narration was a letter home to his mother of the casualties of war— all that he had seen and all that she had taught him in preparation for the world. He ended by saying, 'but mother, you forgot to tell me about Jesus!"

This is also the year that Stevie Wonder did the Concert at the Omni— "They say that heaven is, ten zillion light years away... Where is your God!... And I say, it's taking Him so long, cause we've got so far to come. But in my heart I can feel it... Feel His Spirit..."■

An Invitation to Study Bible Thursdays, 6:30 pm
mustardseedfaith@bellsouth.net

October 19, 2007

Faith of a mustard seed
by Barbara Woods-Washington, M. Div.

I am in receipt of a gift of tools for seeing The Word of God as some of the world's most learned theologians. The gift of interpretation of scripture is from God and my grandmama used to sing about, "what the world didn't give...". It is at this level that I have sought to pass on this gift. So before going forward to the use of pistis/faith in Mark, some have asked to go further into previous columns. So here we go.

"On behalf of The Howard Thurman Educational Trust an invitation to participate in A Seven Day Intensive Seminar discussion with me on The Grounds and The Meaning of Religious Experience."

My initial column referenced a letter that I pulled out of my mailbox and has a date of September 11, 1979. I am so tempted to talk the remainder of this Column about Dr. Thurman— but only to recommend to anyone who has not yet come to know him, his autobiography *"With Head and Heart"*.

'Religious Experience', he said, 'take the time out of your personal and private lives and come and sit with me for seven days while we ponder what is rock bottom, what does it mean— Religious Experience?' And— 'I'll pay for it!' It is a scholarship, a reward— for your commitment to faith.

One of the pieces he submitted is called the "Keeper of The Kinds" which served to bring us to how great the religious experience is in creation. Tree-hood, Tree-kind. Penguin-hood, Penguin-Kind (he collected penguins with

Barbara Woods Riles Washington

"The Voice Of A Proud Community"
Nashville P*R*I*D*E
Pulpit, Pew and Public

☦ 33

conversation about how 'religious the penguin').

I also made reference in the initial column to a concept known as 'de-mythologizing grandmother'. It is an ideology that found it's way into the Biblical Studies classrooms that has to do with the 'myth of grandmother'. It aims at the role of 'faith-keeper of grandma' in (but certainly not exclusive to) the Black Community.

I have a plaque that reads, "God could not be everywhere, so he created grandmothers" which basically says it all. It is directed towards the family in which children have been raised by a grandmother who was responsible for the transmission of faith. I went there with them as one whose grandmother was, in fact, the second parent in the home. A grandmother whose faith in God fed and clothed us on a daily basis. A grandmother whose teachings last far beyond a single lifetime. A grandmother whose memory continues to provide meaning to 'eternal life'. And so because there is not space and time here to further state the reality of 'grandmama's myth', I referenced it to say I "knew church" because of all the church(s) my grandmother took me to in the weighty matter of 'passing on faith'. The 'transmission of faith' to a 'new generation'—a task that 'fell' or was 'appointed' to grandma. They say, we think she 'Is God'. I say, 'she does have wings!' ■

An Invitation to Study Bible Thursdays, 6:30 pm
mustardseedfaith@bellsouth.net

November 2, 2007

Faith of a mustard seed
by Barbara Woods-Washington, M. Div.

The reference made to Howard Thurman's *Epilogue* to **Jesus and the Disinherited** gets to the heart of what I believe to be perhaps the most important task that a religious life has before it: to 'emerge articulate'. Dr. Thurman suggests that when one emerges with a name and character against the forces of history... he has emerged articulate.

In most every course that I have taught, my initial lecture is to bring the group to consciousness of time. I do this by calling attention to our grave marker which for most of us will only identify our name and time in history. This discussion centers around the fact that masses of the world's persons will come and go in history with no evidence of their ever having lived. Some totally unknown, buried in the 'Potter's Field(s)'. There is talk that my grandmother died broken hearted about the fact that her son, my uncle Buddy, Ozzie Smith, a World War II veteran, left her house one day to never be heard from again. She very aggressively hounded authorities as to his whereabouts and was finally told, not long before her passing, that he had been found dead and with no identification on him, he is buried in the Cleveland Potter's Field.

Some who are buried by their loved ones, lay in unmarked graves and very soon forgotten. Some at best have a life marker placed in stone with the 'Three' statistics that identify their space in time for the next generations who seek them: Name, Birth date, the infamous 'Dash' and Date of Demise.

It is 'The Dash', then, that determines the articulated life.

Barbara Woods Riles Washington

☦ 34

The Voice Of A Proud Community
Nashville P*R*I*D*E
Pulpit, Pew and Public

This discussion is also aimed at convincing the student that 'time is wasted on the young' as the old wise tale states. It is no small thing that the 'master', the 'expert', the 'gold metal' of the field is gained by the person who most often starts the task in their childhood. Most of us spend far too many years of our lives pursuing the mundane. When consciousness comes, it then becomes a race— realizing now that 'time is winding up!' It is the one who 'in all their getting, gets understanding' who emerges articulate.

This initial course discussion is not complete without raising the consciousness of 'The Autobiography'. An 'articulated life' is able to raise the interest of others in writing about 'their Dash'— bio/life, graphia/writing. The Biography can only gather information 'about you' with conclusions drawn being in line with what takes place in the legal systems' court rooms, EVIDENTIARY! Yet, in many cases, so far from the truth. You and you alone, can provide 'the truth' of who and what your life's statement is.

Just before my mother's passing, I sat at her bedside and said to her, "Mama, do you realize that you have never told me anything about you? Everything I know about you, someone else told me!" She took her Auto/SELF, bio/LIFE, graphia/WRITING to the grave with her leaving 'Her Dash' to remain the 'oral property' of those who witnessed her life.■

An Invitation to Study Bible Thursdays, 6:30 pm mustardseedfaith@bellsouth.net

November 09, 2007

Faith of a mustard seed
by Barbara Woods-Washington, M. Div.

The column of April 13th drew quite a bit of discussion. The thesis statement is this: "In the 'articulation of faith' process one must come to terms with 'word'."

Because there is a natural tendency to put a definite article with 'word', the paper's editor did just that. I want to look again at 'word' in it's singular form and it's importance to the life of faith.

It is the 'unarticulated life'— (most normally the childhood, adolescence to youth) who allows the use of 'words' to provoke violence. One word is spoken. The response to that word is spoken. A series of words are exchanged (most often of the expletive '4 letter' kind) resulting in an eruption of violence. The wisdom saying evolved— "it is not what you are called, it is what you answer to!" You give power or render powerless 'words'.

Barbara Woods Riles Washington

Even in the Church's Sunday School and Bible Study classes, (many of which have a hovering threat of violence in any given session,) one's word is under attack— all while present here in this setting is One Lord, One Faith and One Baptism!

I recall a class discussion in Seminary from the course "Mission of The Church" when Professor George Thomas stated that "there is only one word that has power to move one to immediate action— the word: GOD. In my persuasion of this, I have very deliberately grown towards hearing a persons 'word association' before processing it's meaning— good, bad or indifferent to my word. An 'articulated life' can most readily receive another's 'word', AND say, "it doesn't mean that

✝ 35

"The Voice Of A Proud Community"
Nashville P*R*I*D*E
Pulpit, Pew and Public

for me!" I cannot, must not invalidate your 'word' in order to give validity to mine. "If your word/logos is not received", Jesus says, not an eruption of violence, "kick the dust off your feet, and move on to the next town!"

It's the discipline of Semantics— the science of meanings. It is a practice of Psychology— psyche/mind logy/word, to state a word for you to respond with the first word that comes to your mind. This 'word association' reveals not just how far we are from the 'true meaning of a word', but, what the word has come to mean to me.

Confusion? Yes! A ball of it! For we live in a world that would take 'word' meanings so far beyond the original intent of the word, that violence erupts— everywhere! Calculated distractions from the most important word of life— GOD, in all of it's wide and varied manifestation.

To the child /adolescent /youth I say, if your word/logos is not bios/life (biology), or socios/social order (sociology), or theos/god (theology), or any of the logy disciplines referenced in the April 13th column, then, YOU ARE DISTRACTED. If when you find yourself in a situation where the exchange of 'words' of the mundane kind is heading for an eruption of violence, (not just in the streets, but also in the home), then this distraction could cost you your life.■

An Invitation to Study Bible Thursdays, 6:30 pm mustardseedfaith@bellsouth.net

November 16, 2007

Faith of a mustard seed
by Barbara Woods-Washington, M. Div.

The column of April 20th stated that of the Four components identified by Systematic Theology that must be considered in any theology: Scripture, Tradition, Sources and Experience— Sources is the starting point for me. Who and what we are informed by plays a major role in how we view the world. One's 'Sources' is critical in our times.

Source Criticism as a field of Biblical Studies, developed as a methodology of looking for and at the sources used by the separate and individual writers of scripture. A monumental task for the earliest source scholars, but made easier today by laws of plagiarism— it is illegal to write in our times without crediting one's sources. I recall being addressed by a Bishop in the United Methodist Church on the steps of my alma mater, Gammon Theological Seminary.

Barbara Woods Riles Washington

He inquired of something that someone had told him I said about him. I simply said to him that he should "consider the source!" As the childhood game goes of whispering in the first persons ear and following the information from ear to ear as it reaches the end, the last person's information is completely different from the first. What is not considered in the human process is how information takes on 'motive'. How difficult it is to get 'the truth, the whole truth, and nothing but the truth!'

Perhaps the most difficult problem with sources for us is the massive expansion of media technology, namely— television, radio, newspaper and the most recent phenomenon of internet. Many TV and radio personalities disseminate information orally

☦ 36

"The Voice Of A Proud Community"
Nashville P*R*I*D*E
Pulpit, Pew and Public

on a daily basis, often without the process of research for credibility and authenticity. Persons listen attentively and yet, again without the process of research for credibility, begin to pass the information on as truth. 'Considering sources' also includes 'context' of information. Identifying a source can be just as damaging if the source's 'word' is taken 'out of context'. The 'sin of omission' goes to work.

Written sources— books, newspapers, etc., too, must be processed for credibility. So many persons believe anything that is read simply because it is in print. My Old Testament Literature professor, Dr. G. Murray Branch, required each student to write and do a class presentation on the literary background of an assigned book of OT. Most often than not, upon completion of the presentation his comment was the same "I am tired of you coming in here with these Sunday school sources!" I suspect that we are 'like Mikey— we'll eat anything' when it comes to the apathetic and haphazard way in which we handle sources.■

An Invitation to Study Bible Thursdays, 6:30 pm mustardseedfaith@bellsouth.net

November 23, 2007

Faith of a mustard seed
by Barbara Woods-Washington, M. Div.

The discussion of scripture, a second component of the articulated faith statement, is much like a totem pole— different faces stacked upon each other to form a single unit.

To begin with— language. I am amazed at the 'bible wars' that take place solely based upon the single expression: 'the Bible says...', when our dependence upon English translations render our interpretations soluble. For this reason alone, I believe that each person of faith has the task of knowing the historical context of your chosen translation. Just because it's 'easy to read' does not mean that you reach the depth of scriptural understanding— 'easy is as easy does...'! Motive, too, exists in translation. Truth is lost in translation.

I am constantly reminded that Jesus did not speak English!

Barbara Woods Riles Washington

I am persuaded by the 'Bar Mitzvah' tradition in Judaism as one that is most powerful in the transmission of faith. The 'Twelve Year Old' becomes a 'Son Of The Law' and begins to learn scripture in it's original written language— Old Testament Hebrew. A very vital part of this ritual is the 'drop of honey upon scripture' to indicate to the child/youth now taking on the responsibility of growing into adulthood that 'there is nothing sweeter than the Word/Law of God'. I envision the Christian Church contributing this tradition in the Black community to turn the direction of a lost generation of children/youth. Killing?— 'THOU SHALL NOT!' Stealing...?

The next face on the 'scriptural totem pole', for me

The Voice Of A Proud Community
Nashville P*R*I*D*E
Pulpit, Pew and Public

would be the Biblical Studies field of Literary Criticism. I am reminded of the life long level of commitment that individuals have given to the texts of scripture across the ages. If you have never seen a theological library, stand someday among the stacks and recognize the volume. We so very casually handle scripture one hour on Sunday Morning and maybe one hour during the week. Another face, the canonization process. The council(s) criteria and vote for inclusion into Bible. The value of apocryphal scripture—those which for one reason or another were not included, but kept across the ages with the Bible canon for their truth testaments. The evidence of 'pseudo' authorship of certain books which met the criteria and are included in the Bible canon.

Another face, as you grow 'strong in The Word' is the universality of scripture. During my Chaplaincy at Bennett College, I was selected as a participant in the **Faculty Resource Network Summer Seminar** on *"The Children of Abraham: Judaism, Christianity and Islam"* at New York University. As a Faculty Network Scholar the summer of 1990, I joined with 15 other religious educators from a network of US Colleges and Universities in this three week intensive 8 hr day study with Dr. Frank Peters. Dr. Peters turned over to each of us his then yet unpublished more than 1,000 page manuscript to include a parallel of the commonalities of the scriptures of these three major world religions.

In the very global world— yea, neighborhoods in which we now live, scripture is a 'search of common ground'. It is Tanakh— Torah, Nevi'im, Kethuvim. It is Qur'an and it is Vedas, Upanishads, and Bhagavad Gita. Howard Thurman said to us, "it is not true because it's in the Bible, it's in the Bible because it's true!"■

*An Invitation to Study Bible
Thursdays. 6:30 pm
mustardseedfaith@bellsouth.net*

November 30, 2007

Faith of a mustard seed
by Barbara Woods-Washington, M. Div.

Returning from Cleveland in Eulogizing Theresa Donaldson Willis at her request. Services on yesterday (Wednesday) with a snow that began the night before when I arrived and remained constant throughout the day. I have thought many times that the cemetery is the coldest place on earth. By the service of committal we were greeted by snowflakes the size of hail. Gave thanks to God, some more, for recognizing the fact that I would be like a bird, 'headed south'.

My 'life word' in scripture, again, John 5. Constance Smith Burwell (and I name her because of her kind heartedness) worshiped at St. Phillip's AME Church on TSU's Homecoming Sunday 2006 where I delivered the morning sermon. I've known her since Fall '74 when I held the position of Dress Chair for her pledge line. But, I took the John 5 Text Homecoming Sunday and used as the subject 'Rise In The Imperative'. After service she took me out to see the license plate on her car. My mind was referencing those 'Absolutely Alpha Chi' license plate frames that we received that Saturday at the 70th Anniversary celebration. (That would be a no!) Her plate had one word. It simply said 'RISE'.

The discussion moved on from 'Scripture' to 'Tradition'. The column of May 4th was an introduction to the many denominations of Christendom and how as a faith it has splintered into an innumerable number of churches. A second look at this component of theology draws me into the text of Mark 7, 'The Parable On Defilement'. Here Jesus quotes the prophet Isaiah as it is written

Barbara Woods Riles Washington

"This people honors me with their lips, but their hearts are far from me; in vain do they worship me, teaching as doctrines the precepts of men." He then says, "You leave the commandments of God and hold fast to the traditions of men."

'Paradosis/tradition' is used by Jesus here to indicate the conflict between commandment(God) and tradition (hu/man). It is clear that Jesus' theology is one of less and not more. While humanity has very deliberately concretized translations and interpretations of the commandments giving rise to traditions and disciplines that are sectarian, denominational and divisive in nature; Jesus has simplified the commandments from Ten to Two with a theme that is unitarian in it's message to humanity— Love God; Love Neighbor; and Love Self

I count it a blessing to have been present at the Stevie Wonder Concert here in Nashville last week-end. His message reached it's peak in saying that there is no leader in our world today whose voice is speaking to stop the wars, violence and hate. "Love's in need of love today, don't delay send yours in right away!"■

An Invitation to Study Bible
Thursdays, 6:30 pm
mustardseedfaith@bellsouth.net

December 7, 2007

Faith of a mustard seed
by Barbara Woods-Washington, M. Div.

Revisiting the 'Experience' component of theology, I turn to the 'Conversion Experience', so very personal in nature that the old spiritual says it best— "You don't know what the Lord told me... You don't know, you wasn't there. You can't say when and you can't say where..."

Notable for word study is the concept 'strepho' which in scripture has the meaning 'to turn'; 'to twist'; 'to bend'; 'to change'. It is used in the Old Testament to refer to inner conversion through suffering or fear. After anointing Saul for the Kingship, he is told by Samuel that the Spirit of the Lord would grip him and he would be changed into another man.

Several forms of 'strepho' are used in scripture, here most notably two: 'apostrepho' (apostacy)— 'to turn away from'; 'to turn aside'; 'to turn back'; 'to reject', and, 'epistrepho'— 'to turn one's attention to'; 'to pay regard to'; 'to be intentive'; 'to turn one's heart to'; 'to take up a matter'. Key to the root and most all forms of this word is conscious action. It places this experience time and time again in the very heart of faith as the action relates directly to God. Turning away or turning towards God establishes a relationship that effects how the individual will subsequently experience life and the world in which he lives.

Most recalled in preaching are the conversion experiences of Isaiah and Paul. This single experience of a person's life is spoken of by the worlds greatest theologians as one that so alters, so turns, so twists, so changes the individual's life that 'they will never be the same again!'

Barbara Woods Riles Washington

"The Voice Of A Proud Community"
Nashville P*R*I*D*E
Pulpit, Pew and Public

The 'knowledge/revelation' gained by this experience dictates all future actions on the part of the 'changed man'. The world view of the individual is turned towards truth— in seeking, in living and in propagation.

My birth Church used to sing a song that had an amazing level of participation. They sang— "Oh, oh, oh, oh somebody touched me! (3 times) And it must have been the hand of the Lord." Then they sang a verse for each day of the week— "It was on a Monday when somebody touched me! (3 times) And it must have been the hand of the Lord." Individuals would stand up for the Monday chorus and others would join those standing as each day was called. I remember wondering if and when I was supposed to stand. I knew that whatever they were singing about was so important, so special that each person remembered the very day that it happened to them. Experiencing God in such a way that your life is 'born again! New Life! NEW BIRTHDAY! Jesus says that every person MUST have one!∎

*An Invitation to Study Bible
Thursdays. 6:30 pm
mustardseedfaith@bellsouth.net*

December 14, 2007

Faith of a mustard seed
by Barbara Woods-Washington, M. Div.

In the season of Christmas, I commend to you another book written by Howard Thurman, **'The Mood Of Christmas'**. I have used it over the years for devotionals as well as Christmas card messages.

The opening section is titled *'The Reaches Of The Past'*. In this section is the writing entitled *'The Singing Of Angels'*. Dr. Thurman writes "It is of profoundest significance to me that the Gospel story, particularly in the Book of Luke, reveals that the announcement of the birth of Jesus comes first to simple shepherds who were about their appointed tasks. After theology has done its work, after the reflective judgements of men from the heights and lonely retreats of privilege and security have wrought their perfect patterns, the birth of Jesus remains the symbol of the dignity and inherent worthfulness of the common man." ... "If the theme of the angels' song is to find fulfillment in the world, it will be through the common man's becoming aware of his true worthfulness and asserting his generic prerogatives as a child of God. The diplomats, the politicians, the statesmen, the lords of business and religion will never bring peace to the world. Violence is the behavior pattern of Power in the modern world, and violence has its own etiquette and ritual, and its own morality."

The section *'The Christmas Greeting'* opens with this initial statement, again one that cannot be paraphrased— "The true meaning of Christmas is expressed in the sharing of one's graces in a world in which it is

Barbara Woods Riles Washington

'The Voice Of A Proud Community'
Nashville P*R*I*D*E
Pulpit, Pew and Public

so easy to become callous, insensitive, and hard. Once this spirit becomes part of a man's life, every day is Christmas, and every night is freighted with anticipation of the dawning of fresh, and perhaps holy, adventure."

From the section titled *'Christmas Meditations'*. One Christmas Sunday while Pastor to the Gordon Road Church in Atlanta, I laid out the writing *'The Gift Of Memory'* in a gift box graphic complete with a bow and placed it in the centerfold of the morning Bulletin. This meditation speaks to us as a reminder of how priceless the gift of memory is! After a discussion on the supposition of having no emory, (very real for those who have begun to develop or are caring for parents who are in various stages of Dementia and/or Alzheimer), he raises the question of how we use our memory. Most striking to me is his perception on how we store away the unpleasant experience and every time we encounter that person, it is the first, and sometimes the only thing about them that we recall. "The next time you feel that life is mean or completely evil and that there is no good in it for you or anyone else, try this: make a list of some of the beautiful things you have seen, the breathlessly kind things people have done for you without obligation, the gracious moments that have turned up in the week's encounters." Just to refresh our memory.■

An Invitation to Study Bible Thursdays. 6:30 pm mustardseedfaith@bellsouth.net

---
December 21, 2007

Faith of a mustard seed
by Barbara Woods-Washington, M. Div.

A heavyweight 'on faith' is Paul Tillich and any serious faith based theological study must take into account his work "Dynamics Of Faith". In his introduction he writes, "There is hardly a word in the religious language, both theological and popular, which is subject to more misunderstandings, distortions and questionable definitions than the word "faith." It belongs to those terms which need healing before they can be used for the healing of men." "... the only way of dealing with the problem is to try to reinterpret the word and remove the confusing and distorting connotations, some of which are the heritage of centuries." "... more far-reaching aim to convince some readers of the hidden power of faith within themselves and of the infinite significance of that to which faith is related."

Barbara Woods Riles Washington

This estimation on the misunderstandings and questionable definitions of the word faith can be readily seen in the 'pat' answer given historically by the Christian Church and most every church member. It is a simple recitation of Hebrews Eleven[th] chapter — "Now faith is the substance of things hoped for and the evidence of things not seen." It was not until I studied Hebrews as a course in Seminary under Dr. R. C. Briggs that I came to realize how little the church has transmitted from this book. Most all sermons preached from Hebrews are 'stuck in the Eleventh chapter'! Our knowledge of faith is indeed 'the heritage of centuries' that leaves us with little more than a 'testimony to faith'.

☦ 42

"The Voice Of A Proud Community"
Nashville P*R*I*D*E
Pulpit, Pew and Public

Tillich, in his 're-interpretation' of the word 'faith' opens this hallmark writing with the definition: FAITH AS ULTIMATE CONCERN! Yet more than this— "Faith is the state of being ultimately concerned!" The discussion of 'ultimate concern' moves beyond food, shelter (and clothing) to enter the social and political and religious life. Further, that ultimacy demands surrender and sacrifice to 'the concern'. Two examples are given: one—the religion of the Old Testament; and two—the ultimate concern with "success, social standing and economic power, 'the god' in the highly competitive Western Culture". Once the ultimate concern is identified, it demands that all other concerns be sacrificed.

I continue to be at a loss as to why the future of children in the Black Nashville community (and Cleveland, et al) continues to be in question. School systems are no longer prepared (or are preparing) to meet the needs of this population who remain heirs of genocidal systems. Such a large portion of this population in preparation for penitentiaries— the 'modern American system of slavery'. Ultimate concern for the social life which effect the whole of life!

"Some of these concerns", Tillich writes, "are urgent, often extremely urgent." ■

An Invitation to Study Bible Thursdays, 6:30 pm
mustardseedfaith@bellsouth.net

January 4, 2008

Faith of a mustard seed
by Barbara Woods-Washington, M. Div.

The title alone that Tillich has given this work, **'The Dynamics Of Faith'**, indicates a most important aspect of faith— Faith Is Dynamic!' Where religious history's authoritative forces have sought to formalize faith (and quite successfully as can be seen in the capitalistic state of the modern day church), it must be borne in mind that 'Faith Is Dynamic! As Howard Thurman puts it— around every corner lies a new encounter with God. Faith is Dynamic! With each new day's dawning...

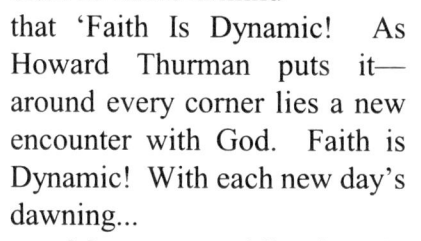

Must tarry awhile, then, in Tillich's section <u>'Faith As A Centered Act'</u> where he writes, "Faith as ultimate concern is an act of the total personality. It happens in the center of the personal life and includes all its elements. Faith is the most centered act of the human mind." "...This makes the psychology of personality highly dynamic and requires a dynamic theory of faith as the most personal of all personal acts."

The discussion centers on several polarities which create tension and conflict by their very nature. The unconscious and the conscious; faith and freedom; ego and superego; the ecstatic and the rational; cognitive and emotion.

In my birth church, shouting was a free will way of worship. No nurses, no ushers functioning as 'prohibitors' of spiritual and emotional acts of faith. No water, no fans, no 'holding of hands to form a constraining barrier???' around an ecstatic act of faith. Just the free will outpouring of faith in worship happening at the very 'center of the personal life and including all its elements'. As a child, it

Barbara Woods Riles Washington

✝ 43

"The Voice Of A Proud Community"
Nashville P*R*I*D*E
Pulpit, Pew and Public

scared me to be in the midst of this worship and I recall my grandmother saying to me in my fright, "nobody ever got hurt in the spirit!"

Now, it scares me when I enter a church that has established a tradition to include an entire team of nurses dressed with capes, hats and all. A conflict for me that the dynamics of faith at work in the personal life in worship has become a 'formalized' treatment as illness. Looking at some of the 'worship nurses' (and ushers with fans and water; and 'ring barriers') I'm thinking you could use a good 'spiritual movement' in you! You might hear me crying out, "you can't put that fire out! It's a Holy Ghost fire! Let it burn! Let it burn!" I can say to the one who is experiencing a dynamic act of faith, "Receive power! Receive power! The world can't give it. The world can't take it. Hallelujah. Glory Hallelujah." Faith is dynamic.

Can't go without a statement Tillich makes in discussing the polarity of 'faith and freedom' where he has a logic line conclusion that "faith IS freedom". Jesus said it— "whom the Son sets free is free indeed."■

*An Invitation to Study Bible Thursdays, 6:30 pm
mustardseedfaith@bellsouth.net*

January 11, 2008

Faith of a mustard seed
by Barbara Woods-Washington, M. Div.

Using the text of Matthew 10:1, Paul Tillich preached a sermon, recorded in his work entitled **'The New Being'** (1955). *"And he called to him his twelve disciples and gave them authority over unclean spirits to cast them out, and to heal every disease and every infirmity."* He uses a simple subject: *'On Healing'*.

Barbara Woods Riles Washington

He opens by recounting a recent three month trip to Germany where he saw a 'sick people'. A people whose faces, as a whole and as individuals, were shaped by 'burdens too heavy to be carried', 'sorrows too deep to be forgotten'. Living with anxieties, confusions, self-contradictions, guilt-feelings. Hiding under denials, accusations of others, hostility, self-pity and self-hate.

Returning home to American to his post, at the time, as Professor of Philosophy and Religion at Union Theological Seminary in Harlem, he questioned the 'appearance of a healthy people'— "we hear that of all illnesses, mental illness is by far the most wide spread in this country. What does this mean?" "...There may be something in the structure of our institutions which produces illness in more and more people."

He suggests a look at 'ruthless competition' which deprives of security— not only in the unsuccessful! On to the harshness of an insecure life and the choosing of mental illness as a place of flight. Fleeing into situations where 'real life' cannot touch. "Don't underestimate this temptation... ...It is human heritage and it is increased immensely by our present world."

The Voice Of A Proud Community
Nashville P*R*I*D*E
Pulpit, Pew and Public

☦ 44

I have on numerous occasions gone to the Men's Shelter in Nashville to drive some of these men to job sites, several of whom I have come to know by name and life story. Such a large and ever growing population. These men are fathers, sons, brothers, husbands who even these relationships are not enough to bring them back from their situations of life abandonment— 'real life can't touch them here!'

'Real life?' Easy for us to say. Real life for many of them is the unjust legal and penal systems; and institutions that will not allow for them a 'real life.' Burdens too heavy to be carried, sorrows too deep to be forgotten. Living with anxieties, confusions, self-contradictions, guilt-feelings. Hiding under denials, accusations of others, hostility, self-pity and self-hate. Not to mention the smell... the smell... the smell of homelessness which those of us with so-called 'real life' find most offensive.

Tillich's 'Kingdom Point' in this message includes this faith statement: "Faith does not mean the belief in assertions for which there is no evidence. It never meant that in genuine religion and it never should be abused in this sense. But faith means being grasped by a power that is greater than we are, a power that shakes us and turns us, and transforms us and heals us." Those feeling threats of existence, Jesus gave them back to themselves— as new creatures.■

An Invitation to Study Bible Thursdays. 6:30 pm
mustardseedfaith@bellsouth.net

January 18, 2008

Faith of a mustard seed
by Barbara Woods-Washington, M. Div.

In revisiting **'The New Being'**, Tillich takes the text of Romans 8:38-39 where Paul writes what Tillich says are "among the most powerful ever written"— *"For I am sure that neither death, nor life, nor angels, nor principalities, nor things present, nor things to come, nor powers, nor height, nor depth, nor anything else in all creations, will be able to separate us from the love of God in Christ Jesus our Lord."* Based on this scripture, Tillich uses the subject— <u>'Principalities and Powers'</u>

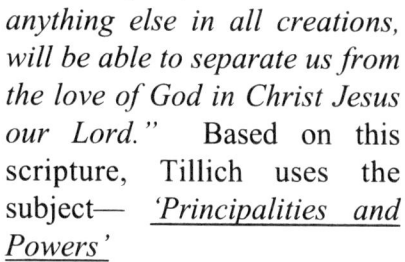

This message centers on the powers named in this text which all men of all the world's histories have been in bondage to. Each one of us held sway by these insoluble conflicting forces. No security is guaranteed to anyone. Tribulation, distress, persecution, famine, nakedness— those powers with evil names. But then, the discussion turns to powers that have 'glorious names'— 'angels', 'principalities', 'life', 'height'. Tillich suggests that these are the most threatening to life because they have a 'double face'. "They grasp us by the good they bring and they destroy us by the evil they contain." As one example, he names "one of these powers with an angelic face is love."

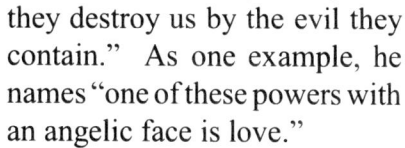

This past Saturday I spoke a word to the Payne Chapel AME Church's Drillteam at their First (Annual) Banquet. I have watched them grow as a children's ministry and can bear witness to it being one of the better ministries to Youth and Children in the city of Nashville. I selected as scripture another

Barbara Woods Riles Washington

✝ 45

"The Voice Of A Proud Community"
Nashville P*R*I*D*E
Pulpit, Pew and Public

passage from Romans, (12:9) to say to them— "let love be genuine. Hate what is evil. Hold fast to what is good."

The faith statement Tillich makes in this message is this, "Faith in Providence is faith altogether. It is the courage to say yes to one's own life and life in general, in spite of the driving forces of fate, in spite of the insecurities of daily existence, in spite of the catastrophes of existence and the breakdown of meaning."

His 'Kingdom point' is a discussion on the 'nor anything else in all creation...'. That all these powers, all these principalities are 'creations' which, just as you and I are creations— are subject to the will of The Creator! Divine Providence!

I too, think that this Romans text is Paul greatest work— to remind us that all these things separate us from the love of God. Yet, not without the power to 'conquer through Christ Jesus, Our Lord'. Gladys Knight sang it first, "I've had my share of life's ups and downs", but James Cleveland and Charles Fold raised it to Kingdom level in identifying 'The Best Thing That Ever Happened To Me' as Jesus.■

An Invitation to Study Bible
Thursdays. 6:30 pm
mustardseedfaith@bellsouth.net

January 25, 2008

Faith of a mustard seed
by Barbara Woods-Washington, M. Div.

"Let the prophet who has a dream tell the dream, but let him who has my word speak my word faithfully. What has straw in common with wheat? Says the Lord. Is not my word like fire, says the Lord, and like a hammer which breaks the rock in pieces? Therefore, behold, I am against the prophets, says the Lord, who steal my words from one another. Behold, I am against the prophets, says the Lord, who use their tongues and say, "Says The Lord." "...Then Zedekiah the king asked Jeremiah secretly in his house and said: "Is there any word from the Lord?" (Jeremiah 23:28-31; 37:17)

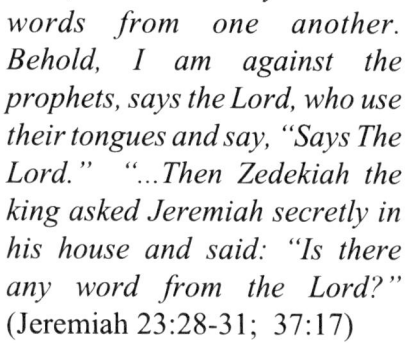

Tillich, again in **'The New Being'**, using the subject *'Is There Any Word From The Lord?'*, examines this text of Jeremiah in the context of faith. The discourse indicates that this question has been asked historically by 'kings in moments of danger'; by 'people in times of unrest'; by 'individuals in moments of great personal decision'. Situations of helplessness and hopelessness.

This week in Nashville amidst a very unusual cold snap of into the second week of below freezing temperatures, a young (black) male's failure at fathering his year old son and two year old daughter came to light with the death of his son. He arrived at the hospital emergency room with the children malnourished and their body temperatures far below the normal state. The news reported their living condition as an apartment with no electricity and no food with the deceased child weighting 10 lbs. The neighbors interviewed had varying degrees

Barbara Woods Riles Washington

"The Voice Of A Proud Community"
Nashville P*R*I*D*E
Pulpit, Pew and Public

✝ 46

of comments to include the 'shouldas' and the 'couldas', not to forget the 'wouldas'. The authorities responded by— 'locking him up' and 'pressing charges!' IS THERE ANY WORD FROM THE LORD?

In the moments of danger, the times of unrest, and the circumstances of great personal decision, the possibilities (to include loss) are unsettling. The consequences of proposed actions (including non action) are disturbing. Even the 'hind sighted wouldas' offer no real "liberation from the longing that grows in the soul." IS THERE ANY WORD FROM THE LORD? This question, when and where asked, elevates the situation to 'ultimate importance' and 'infinite significance'. In doing so, among other things, the anxiety is removed and courage is given.

"The Church and it's servants," Tillich suggests, (have made the Word From The Lord) "a matter of law and tradition, of habit and convention." A possession. That no longer cuts into 'our ordinary world. A possession. Of something that can NEVER BE possessed! Ceasing to ask and to cry out for It... IS THERE ANY WORD FROM THE LORD? ■

An Invitation to Study Bible Thursdays. 6:30 pm mustardseedfaith@bellsouth.net

February 1, 2008

Faith of a mustard seed
by Barbara Woods-Washington, M. Div.

Jesus said, "For judgment I came into this world, that those who do not see may see, and that those who see may become blind." Some of the Pharisees near him heard this, and they said to him, "Are we also blind?" Jesus said to them, "If you were blind, you would have no guilt; but now that you say, 'We see,' your guilt remains." (John 9:39-41). One last look at Tillich's **'The New Being'** before returning to scripture to the use of faith/pistis in Mark's Gospel. This message he titles *'Seeing And Hearing'*.

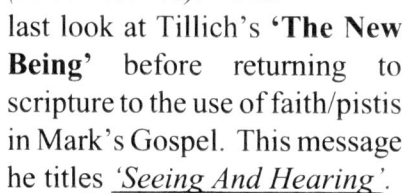

The discourse begins with a statement of the fact that both Biblical Testaments, and most religious literature speaks consistently of seeing: 'come and see'; 'we have seen'; 'everyone who sees the son'. "It is not true that religious faith is belief in things without evidence. The word 'evidence' means 'seeing thoroughly'. And we are asked to see." Isaiah is noted as being the greatest of all prophets "after he had seen God in the Temple". Jesus' blessing upon 'the pure in heart' identifies the "ultimate fulfillment, the end of all moving and striving... the eternal vision of God."

Barbara Woods Riles Washington

Noting the long struggle that the historical Church had with 'seeing and hearing', the homily now recognizes that 'hearing' won the battle during the Reformation when the Church became centered around the 'preacher's desk'— "Hearing replaced seeing, obedience replaced vision."

Most significant for me is this statement— "Seeing is the most astonishing of our natural powers. It receives the light, the first of all that is created, and as the light does it conquers

† 47

The Voice Of A Proud Community
Nashville P*R*I*D*E
Pulpit, Pew and Public

darkness and chaos." Making these points: seeing creates; seeing unites and seeing goes beyond itself.

The late great homiletics professor, Dr. Isaac R. Clark in his course 'Delivery of Sermons' developed this process for critiquing sermon delivery. Tasked with three scheduled sermon deliveries, you stood at the 'preacher's desk' facing the class as critics. In addition to facing a two-way mirrored back wall which, although you couldn't see him, you knew that Dr. Clark was on the other side. Shortly into your first round sermon he would burst through the door waving a red flag—"Shut up, fool!" He had a peculiar way of 'seeing beyond what he was hearing'. When Clark alumni gather we don't know of anyone who made it through the first round of sermon delivery.

The discourse continues by pointing to innumerable temples and churches throughout the world's history that contain 'things' and 'images' —idols which hold us fast to themselves and do not lead us beyond. We enter in self-surrender but leave empty and in despair.

"Perhaps we want to deprive ourselves of our eyes like Œdipus, of our eyes which first did not see what they ought to see and now cannot stand to see what they must see." I see men who look like trees ...∎

An Invitation to Study Bible Thursdays, 6:30 pm mustardseedfaith@bellsouth.net

---
February 8, 2008

Faith of a mustard seed
by Barbara Woods-Washington, M. Div.

Much is said about Mark's Gospel as it has become for the field of New Testament not simply 'the center' Gospel but 'The First' written of The Three 'Synoptic Gospels'.

The urgency of Mark is an easily identifiable theme where the word 'immediately' can be seen eight times in just the first chapter. Perhaps the Church's birthing in an environment of persecution solely accounts for the urgency of it's message. The Church in our times has lost it's urgency. We no longer await— the true 'Great Expectation'— the coming of The Lord. It is here that we can begin to look at the use of 'faith/pistis' in Mark.

Young's Analytical Concordance records only five uses of faith/pistis in Mark and, as in Matthew, this word is used within the realm of healing. First is this Triple Tradition pericope on **'The Healing Of The Paralytic'** (Mark 2:1-12).

Synoptic variations from Matthew's account (Matt 9:1-18) include Caperneum as the locale and preaching as His activity— to an overflowing crowd. Four men carry the paralytic and, unable to get near Him, they remove the roof to lower the pallet.

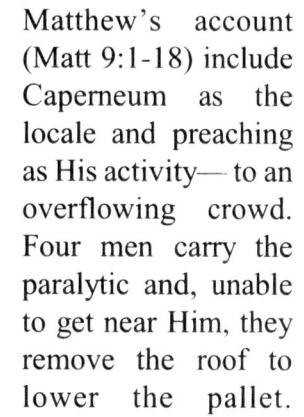

'Immediately' Jesus perceived the questioning of the scribes. The paralytic rose and 'immediately' took up his pallet. The response of those gathered— "we never saw anything like this!"

Gunther Bornkamm, one of my very favorite New Testament theologians makes this statement, "In the tradition of Jesus' sayings faith is always linked with power and miracle. ...Where Jesus does not find this faith, he cannot work a miracle.

Barbara Woods Riles Washington

☦ 48

"The Voice Of A Proud Community"
Nashville P*R*I*D*E
Pulpit, Pew and Public

...What matters here, however, is the readiness to receive the miracle."

I am reminded that of all the hospital visits that I made during my pastoral service at Salem, I shall forever remember the look on Trustee Ruby Reeves face on her way to major surgery. I have looked upon more sickness than I can begin to recall, but Ruby had this angelic glow about her as she said to me "it's in God's hands!" Never saw anything like this! When she returned to church as though 'something' had happened, I know for certain that her faith had made her whole!

Key to our re-defining faith here is the fact that in the synoptic use of faith it is 'already there'! Faith is a prerequisite to healing! It is not a 'seeing is believing' or a 'show me state' of life, but, I expect you to, I know you can. "All who turn to him in faith count on the power of Jesus which knows no bounds, and on the miracle which he can work, where all human help fails."

Time and time again, as here with the 'Healing of The Paralytic' Jesus saw 'faith' and responded to this faith with 'healing'. ■

An Invitation to Study Bible Thursdays. 6:30 pm
mustardseedfaith@bellsouth.net

February 15, 2008

Faith of a mustard seed
by Barbara Woods-Washington, M. Div.

Second in Mark's use of 'pistis/faith' is another Triple Tradition pericope— **'The Stilling of The Storm'**, (Mark 4:35-41). Matthew variates from Mark at these points: Mark identifies the great storm with 'wind'; Jesus is asleep on a 'cushion'; and, significant I think, is seen in the variation of questioning. In the dialogue with the disciples Mark records a series of questions where Matthew has exclamations. Noteworthy is the initial question asked in Mark when the disciples woke Jesus saying, "do you not care if we perish?" Here, Matthew records the exclamation, "Save Lord, we are perishing!" (Matt 8:23-27).

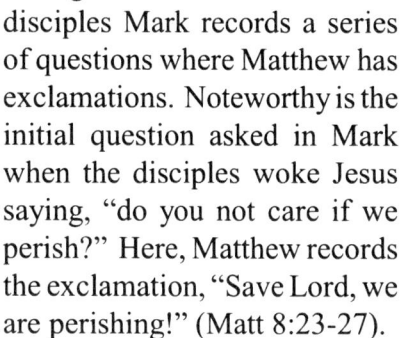

On the variation of 'the cushion', I am immediately reminded of Dr. Thurman's dialogue when he said to us "Jesus Is A Cushion!". In our seven day Educational Trust scholars' seminar, he was in a discussion on some very relevant differences between Judaism and Christianity. He recalled how Jacob wrestled with an angel in saying that Judaism is a faith that the believer has a very personal relationship with God. Face to face. One on one. You can't go God, until you bless me. He likened Jesus' position in Christianity to a 'cushion'. Christians, he said, have put Jesus in the middle, like a cushion.

The 'Stilling of the Storm' is classified a 'miracle story' and appears in Mark as a test of faith— particularly with the doubting mood that the disciples are in. Their mixed emotions come through in that they obviously believe that Jesus has the 'power to know' of the wind storm even 'in his sleep'. That perhaps he should have known

Barbara Woods Riles Washington

"The Voice Of A Proud Community"
Nashville P*R*I*D*E
Pulpit, Pew and Public

† 49

enough to wake up and save them. Or, he simply did not care. "Do you not care if we perish?" In my 'ole preacher's mind's eye', I can see the disciples round table discussion while Jesus is asleep. Surely their very foundation was shaking in the midst of this storm. As their fright turned to resentment that Jesus could even sleep through this, I can hear— "we 'bout to perish"; "He don't care." "It's time for Him to wake up!" "Yeah, we 'bout to go get Him up!"

Unlike Matthew's account where the discussion of fear and faith is the first order of business, in Mark Jesus rebukes the wind at first consciousness. As a response to their fear and lack of faith, but most importantly, I think— a response to their doubt about him caring for them, when he awakes he says first, "Peace. Be Still". It is not just the winds, not just the rains, not just the sea— but also the disciples who are now at peace!

You gotta love a Lord who alone can give you peace in the midst of a storm, yet in your stillness speak a word to question your fear and your lack of faith. Seemed kinda silly to the disciples who now says, "who is this..."■

An Invitation to Study Bible Thursdays. 6:30 pm mustardseedfaith@bellsouth.net

February 22, 2008

Faith of a mustard seed
by Barbara Woods-Washington, M. Div.

Third in Mark's use of 'faith/pistis' is a 3rd Triple Tradition— **'A Woman's Faith'** which is never separate from 'Jairus' Daughter' because the woman's encounter with Jesus is while he and Jairus are en route to see Jairus' daughter. (Mark 5:21-43).

The variations from Matthew include the fact that Mark has given a far more detailed account than Matthew's abbreviated form. (Matthew 9:18-26). Jairus is identified by Mark as a 'ruler of the synagogue', and, while Matthew records Jairus saying to Jesus, "my daughter has just died"; Mark records him saying, "my little daughter is at the point of death". Subsequently, the petition to Jesus in Matthew is for 'resurrection', while in Mark it is for 'healing from sickness unto death'. On 'The Woman's Faith' additional variations include Mark's reporting her great suffering under many physicians— spending all that she had as she was no better but rather grew worse; that she had heard the reports about Jesus; Jesus perceiving that power had gone forth from him; and, where Matthew records Jesus saying to her "take heart, your faith has made you well", Mark records Jesus saying "daughter, your faith has made you well, go in peace, and be healed of your disease".

It was the practice at Salem for the Associate Pastor to vacation the month of July and the Senior Pastor to vacation the month of August. I recall my first August Sunday with total worship leadership responsibility. The largest seating capacity church in Harlem, NYC with a more than

Barbara Woods Riles Washington

The Voice Of A Proud Community
Nashville P*R*I*D*E
Pulpit, Pew and Public

1,000+ worship attendance; a then (1985) paid $30,000 choir to include six paid soloists, some of whom sang on Broadway, with the Minister of Music's name credited in the movie "A Chorus Line" processing before me— feeling demonic forces inhabiting the sanctuary, it is perhaps the most 'faint-hearted' situation of my life. As I mounted the additional step to the elevated pulpit side of the split chancel, I began by reminding the congregation of my consciousness of the dollars spent on our weekly printing of the bulletin (off to Hunt's Printing every Thursday)— therefore it's value; but that today I wanted them to place it inside their Bibles while I deviate from the 'established order'. I explained to the church that 'something is in this house this morning that is not of God'. I asked that each join the hand of the other and the 'order of this day is exorcism'. And when I got through praying, we came up shouting. Nobody doubting! I felt so clearly the moment during the prayer that 'Jesus perceived that power had gone forth from him'. Who touched me? Who touched me?

The disciples said Lord there's a whole crowd of people! Yet, Jesus knew that an insignificant unnamed women came, interrupting, intruding, interfering, intervening in his business with the ruler of the synagogue with faith to access healing power.

And peace? Wish I had the time to talk about the relationship seen here between faith/pistis and peace/eirene. "Go", Jesus told the woman of faith, "in peace"!■

An Invitation to Study Bible Thursdays. 6:30 pm
mustardseedfaith@bellsouth.net

February 29, 2008

Faith of a mustard seed
by Barbara Woods-Washington, M. Div.

Fourth of five uses of 'pistis/faith' by Mark is a 4th Triple Tradition known as **'The Healing of Bartimaeus'**. Still again, faith and healing are one. (Mark 10:46-52).

Mark variates from Matthew where Matthew records the encounter was with two blind men (Matt 20:29-34), neither of which are named. Mark identifies a lone man as Bartimaeus, the blind beggar, son of Timaeus. Mark's account alone in the triple include Jesus sending followers to call Bartimaeus and they say to him, *"take heart; rise, he is calling you. And throwing off his mantle he sprang up and came to Jesus."* It is also significant to note that for Matthew this is not a 'faith encounter'—where the healing of the blind men was out of pity. A final note of redaction— Mark alone records Jesus saying to Bartimaeus, *"go your way..."*

Barbara Woods Riles Washington

I have resisted the temptation to place handles on the word of faith as it has continued to come weekly for the appointed task in writing this column. As Dr. Thurman would say when we offered commentary, "you put the handle on it!" But here, 'blind beggar' gives me a handle that I must wrestle with in giving incarnation to this word. For some strange reason, blind beggar' is imaging, right now for me, 'my people'. I'm daring to put this handle on this word. I see our blindness in not seeing, (fighting— Ali: "you can't hit what you can't see?") the massive forms of oppression and poverty; this systematic downtrodding of the 'backs upon which this country was built'. Sure, individuals have gained freedom in all of it's capitalistic definitions, but

---

☦ 51

"The Voice Of A Proud Community"
Nashville P*R*I*D*E
Pulpit, Pew and Public

where is 'community' in all of this? Left with a hope of 'lottery' or perhaps 'an extreme make-over' or perhaps 'the Big Give-away'— are these not all forms of begging? Michelle Obama is under heavy criticism, but I think that she has something when she suggests a 'come out of corporate America' and a 'return to community service/building work'. Don't be fooled by the attempts (as always) to destroy the character of any of our leaders who, as 'the messenger' —comes to open our eyes. They want to talk about how much money she makes in her community service position, but, as we come to 'see' this 'new fact'— 'you must be a millionaire to campaign, let alone be elected president of the United States!'. How else could we hear from her!

What most traditional versions translate as *'cloak'*, Bartimaeus threw off— his 'himation/mantle' and *'sprung up'*. Whether it was his identifying Jesus as the 'Son of David' or his readiness to receive healing, I can't say, but, Jesus saw his faith!

I recall as a child in my earliest school days that fights occurred on the school's playground. There was no use of weapons, only the taking off of your coat, 'springing up' to assume the boxing position with both fists up— "come on!"■

An Invitation to Study Bible Thursdays. 6:30 pm mustardseedfaith@bellsouth.net

March 7, 2008

Faith of a mustard seed
by Barbara Woods-Washington, M. Div.

The 5th and final occurrence of 'pistis/faith' in Mark's Gospel is the pericope known as **'The Meaning Of The Withered Fig Tree'** (Mark 11:20-25). It is the first and only Double Tradition of the five and is shared by Matthew where Luke is silent.

Barbara Woods Riles Washington

Variations include Mark's account identifying Peter as the disciple who raised the question about the fig tree. The mood of Peter is reflected by his saying to Jesus, *"...the tree which you cursed..."* as it invokes a response of command— *"Have faith in God!"*; where in Matthew, Jesus' response is subjunctive— *..."if you have faith in God..."* (Matt 21:20-22; 6:14). In addition, Mark's account relates prayer, believing, receiving and forgiveness to faith in giving meaning to the withered fig tree.

'Jesus' Idea Of God' has become a sub section of Rudolf Bultmann's chapter titled *'The Message of Jesus'* in his hallmark work **'Theology Of The New Testament'**. Here he draws attention to Jesus standing in the tradition of 'prophetic consciousness' where the sovereignty of God, the absoluteness of His will, determines man's relativity, relationship and decisions about his world. For Jesus, God is 'Creator/Governor' of the World— 'consider the lilies of the fields...He clothes them all!'. "All anxious care, all haste to get goods to insure life, is therefore senseless— yes, wicked." Bultmann further recognizes that in the common piety of Jesus' Judaism, 'faith in God the Creator' had weakened and "His sway over the(ir) present could barely still be made out".

Peter has, in a mood (attitude?) that is difficult to

"The Voice Of A Proud Community"
Nashville P*R*I*D*E
Pulpit, Pew and Public

describe, called Jesus' attention to 'the tree which he cursed'. What is clear is that he is distracted. With no hesitation, without identifiable correlation, Jesus' response is one of 'prophetic consciousness'— *"Have faith in God"*. A very sobering redirection of Peter's mind, heart and soul. It is significant to note C. F. Mann's commentary that the phrase *'have faith in God'* is found nowhere else.

'Prophetic consciousness' in our times leads me to recognize that, still again, 'faith in God' has so weakened that His sway over our present can barely be made out. The distractions hold us sway drowning out the sobering, redirecting voice speaking the word— HAVE FAITH IN GOD! It occurs to me that Christian theology has served to further weaken this word in that we have made Jesus God; and in our times of 'constant distraction' the need is never more greater to 'know Jesus', but to 'KNOW GOD!' As a single biblical recording, Jesus says to Peter, in his distraction, not have faith in me(Jesus)— HAVE FAITH IN GOD! ■

An Invitation to Study Bible Thursdays, 6:30 pm mustardseedfaith@bellsouth.net

---

March 14, 2008

Faith of a mustard seed
by Barbara Woods-Washington, M. Div.

"My house shall be called a house of prayer for all the nations? But you have made it a den of robbers." Significant to the dynamics of faith is the fact that the study of Mark's 5th and final occurrence of 'pistis/faith' would come forth on the week that is traditionally know by the Church as 'Palm Sunday'. For it is recorded in the 11th chapter which opens with the Palm Sunday narrative. 'The Passion' with which Jesus responds to Peter in this faith encounter is one that must not go under estimated— *"Have faith in God!... So I tell you, whatever you ask for in prayer,..."* (Mark 11:20-25).

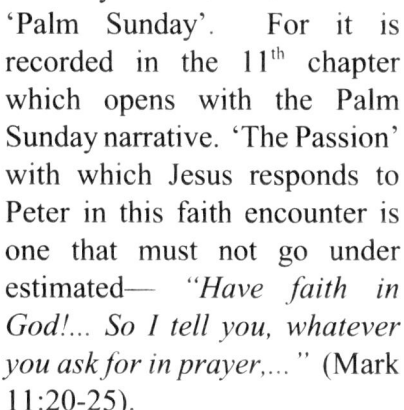

With no less than six different words used in New Testament scripture for the single English translation 'prayer', in this text Jesus uses 'proseuchomai'. From it's very first usage, 'proseuchomai'

Barbara Woods Riles Washington

means 'calling on God'— where other prayer translated words are not clear to whom the request is directed. Those theologians who have closely regarded the various 'prayer' word usages have seen that 'proseuchomai' is a prayer that has a conscious distinction in content. Greeven sees it's rare usage in secular Greek and identifies it's use strictly in Jewish influenced texts.

In my 30 years of ministry having entered the Seminary in 1978, I was forced to come to terms with the confusion surrounding prayer in the Church. I soon learned that as a visitor, I was always called upon, foreknown or just hearing your named called unbeknownst— to do a public Prayer. While I think that the most mis-understood prayer is 'The Invocation' (even now I

☦ 53

'The Voice Of A Proud Community'
Nashville P*R*I*D*E
Pulpit, Pew and Public

find myself as a single solitary individual standing in worship 'to invoke' and 'to receive' the presence of God for worship), I am confused about an order of worship that has no 'Pastoral Prayer'. I recently worshiped for the first time at First Baptist South Inglewood and continue to sing their Pastoral Prayer song which has the melody from 'Blessed Assurance' and speaks saying, "Pray your way through. Pray your way through. God has an answer, Pray your way through!'

"My house shall be called a house of prayer for all the nations? But you have made it a den of robbers." Proseuchomai'— 'calling on God' gets real deep in it's meaning. It is not a request for house, Jesus never had one; nor a petition for money of which he challenged the Church in what it has become. 'Proseuchomai' means 'calling on God'! It is a fact of faith— the presence of God. It is no small thing that Christians have difficulty with a public prayer. The late great Dr. Major J. Jones said in one of his sermons, "If I had my way I would tilt the world and everything would come to me". Prophetic— indeed! But are we prepared to 'call on God'? I think not, because when we stand in His Presence, it is total commitment to 'His Will'— (for all the nations) not mine that shall be done. *"And lo, I will be with you, always..."* ■

An Invitation to Study Bible Thursdays. 6:30 pm mustardseedfaith@bellsouth.net

---

March 21, 2008

Faith of a mustard seed
by Barbara Woods-Washington, M. Div.

"...do not doubt in your heart, but believe that what you say will come to pass,...." Stuck in this fifth and final occurrence of 'pistis/faith' in Mark's Gospel as it continues to reveal dynamics of faith. **'The meaning of The Withered Fig Tree'** must be given extensive attention in light of it's position in this Gospel. (Mark 11:20-25). 'Jesus' Passion' must be seen in giving 'new life' to his sayings that come forth in this the Eleventh (hour) chapter of his life.

The chapter has opened, again, with his 'Triumphant Entry Into Jerusalem' riding on a donkey. While the crowd present at this ride said *"Hosanna! Blessed is he who comes in the name of The Lord"*— Howard Thurman says of him on 'This Ride' that he had come to "feel the sparrowness of the sparrow, the leprosy of the leper, the blindness of the blind, the crippleness of the cripple and the frenzy of the mad." After cursing the fig tree he returned to the Temple where he overturned the 'tables of the money changers'— *"and he would not allow anyone to carry anything through the temple".*

Barbara Woods Riles Washington

Ultimate, I think, of all faith statements ever made is this saying that Jesus gives in His Passion to respond to the beloved disciple's calling his attention to the tree which he cursed— *"Have faith in God. Truly I tell you, if you say to this mountain, 'Be taken up and thrown into the sea,' and if you do not doubt in your heart, but believe that what you say will come to pass, it will be done for you. So I tell you, whatever you ask for in prayer, believe that you have received it, and it will be yours."*

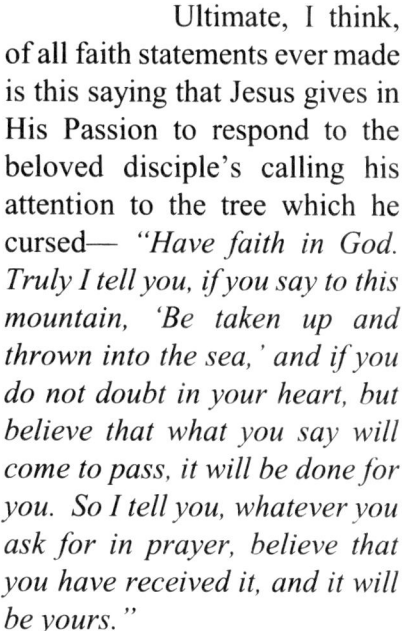

✝ 54

"The Voice Of A Proud Community"
Nashville P*R*I*D*E
Pulpit, Pew and Public

'Diakrino/doubt' is of major importance, in coming to terms with this saying of Jesus. Rooted in 'krino'; used throughout classical Greek in legalism this verb has the meaning: 'to sift'; 'to part'; 'to divide out'; 'to decide'; 'to judge'; 'to dispute'. Translated from Old Testament where it has the theological sense of 'judgement'— both verdict and process. Significant to note that 'crisis' has root in this word— conflict, parting, estrangement. Buchsel suggests that the use of krino as diakrino/doubt is not known prior to the New Testament— "It is specifically religious phenomenon."

Doubt, then, is the 'double-mindedness'; the very nature of modern (hu)man. It involves the 'conflicting motives' of the personal life. The motives, the motives? The Motives! It includes the uncertainty, the insecurities; the 'conflicting doctrines'; science— can anything but dynamite really move a mountain? James is on point, *"the double-minded man IS unstable in all his ways."* For doubt, double-mindedness encompasses the 'upside downwardness' of the wages of good surrounded by 'evil doers! To include vicarious suffering. Not to leave out the 'weapons of mass destruction!'

Key to faith here, then, is that this doubt must not reach the heart! *"For out of the heart comes evil thought, fornication, theft, murder, adultery, wickedness, licentiousness, envy, slander, pride..."* All these things considered, there is only one prayer to be prayed— David at his best, *"Create in me a clean heart!"* ■

An Invitation to Study Bible Thursdays, 6:30 pm mustardseedfaith@bellsouth.net

---

March 28, 2008

Faith of a mustard seed
by Barbara Woods-Washington, M. Div.

'I woke up this morning, I didn't have no doubt! No doubt, no doubt, I didn't have no doubt!' *"Have Faith in God. ... do not doubt in your heart, but believe that you receive..."* Again with **'The Meaning Of The Withered Fig Tree'** Mark's 5th and final occurrence of 'pistis/faith' (Mark 11:20-25).

It must not go unnoticed that 'pisteuete' used by Jesus here for 'believe' is our root word pistis/faith. This gives us, in fact, two different word translations for Jesus' double usage of 'pist-' in Mark's 'The Meaning Of The Withered Fig Tree'. Although we have always somehow known the equivalency of the words faith and believe, here is the now to look closer.

Both active and passive are the senses of faith=belief (pist-) derivatives in Classical Greek. 'Trusting' -'worthy of trust'; 'obedient' -'obey'; 'reliable' - 'rely'; 'certainty'; 'fidelity'; 'confidence'; 'assurance'; 'conviction'; 'dependable truth'; 'firm belief'; 'guarantee'; 'security'; 'contractual relation' are all among the various meanings given in it's usage. Although it never reaches the religious realm, several of the great Philosophers identify faith=belief as "a higher endowment than wealth".

Faith as a religious concept was promoted in Hellenism as the various missionaries identified their deities and demanded faith in them. In this mix, standing strong in a long religious Old Testament heritage for which faith is seen as a 'contractual fear/trust relation to God', Jesus emerges with the diety clearly identified— *"Have Faith in God! Believe in God!"*

Notwithstanding Jesus' foreknowledge of 'Peter's

Barbara Woods
Riles Washington

☦ 55

"The Voice Of A Proud Community"
Nashville P*R*I*D*E
Pulpit, Pew and Public

Denial', what a powerful 'last will and testament' to give the disciple whom he loved. Although Peter was distracted by the withered fig tree, Jesus pricks his consciousness by calling his immediate attention to God— *"Have Faith in God! Believe in God!"* By the double usage, Jesus goes beyond hearing— 'Peter's ears' and moves this saying to 'his mind'— think on this thing— *"Have Faith in God! Believe in God!"* Had this saying reached 'Peter's Heart' (as in John's Gospel where He finally had to say to Peter 3 times— "if you love me, feed my sheep!), the Denial and the return to Fishing might not have come.

I remember with warmth the look on my grandmother's face when she sang this song— "Only believe. Only believe. All things are possible, only believe." I can still feel the power in the affirmation of faith sung in this verse as it took the singing worshiper to a whole other level— "Lord, I believe. "Lord, I believe. All things are possible, Lord, I believe". ■

An Invitation to Study Bible Thursdays. 6:30 pm mustardseedfaith@bellsouth.net

---

April 4, 2008

Faith of a mustard seed
by Barbara Woods-Washington, M. Div.

Then there is the question of 'receiving' giving understanding to Mark's 5th and final occurrence of 'pistis/faith', **'The Meaning Of The Withered Fig Tree'** (Mark 11:20-25). *"So I tell you, whatever you ask for in prayer, believe that you have received it, and it will be yours."*

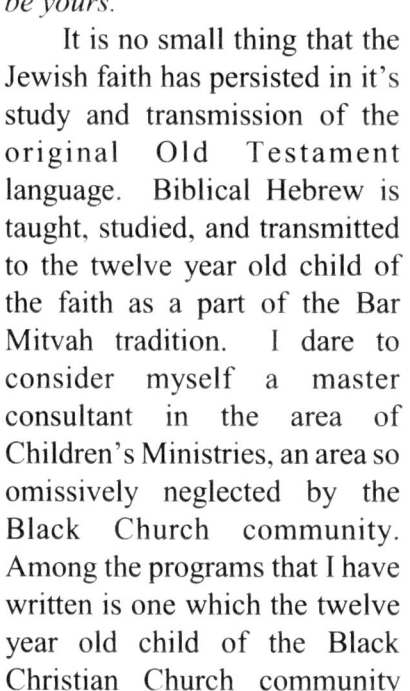

It is no small thing that the Jewish faith has persisted in it's study and transmission of the original Old Testament language. Biblical Hebrew is taught, studied, and transmitted to the twelve year old child of the faith as a part of the Bar Mitvah tradition. I dare to consider myself a master consultant in the area of Children's Ministries, an area so omissively neglected by the Black Church community. Among the programs that I have written is one which the twelve year old child of the Black Christian Church community would participate in an after school Biblical Greek language program. The dependency upon translations and sermon transmission of scripture has given rise to a spiritual impotence.

Barbara Woods Riles Washington

The word 'receive', then, is an excellent example of understanding being lost in translation. So many words in New Testament scripture that English translations all translate using the single word 'receive'. Two of them, lambano and dexomai both have several variations at work in the Gospels— yet we never see anything but the word receive. While dexomai is most often a 'passive' usage of 'receive', lambano is fairly common in New Testament as an 'active' form and has the sense: 'to grasp'; 'to seize'; 'of things that one has a claim to'; 'to collect'; 'to acquire'; 'to lay firm hold of'; 'to cleave to'; 'to bring into one's sphere'; 'to hold fast'; 'to understand'; 'persistent grasp'; 'intensive grasp'. Young references Jesus' usage of 'receive' here as a part of the lambano word family. And yet, the actual word Jesus uses in giving meaning to the withered fig tree is 'elabete' and is found nowhere else!

Apart from New Testament Literary Criticism's finding problems with this verse, look again! Again, Jesus is in 'His Passion'— as His 'last will and testament' it is a most powerful eulogy— 'receiving' (the most rarest form of receiving, in fact) as a (re)action to prayer action!

Dr. R. C. Briggs (who wrote the book on New Testament Interpretation used by many seminarians) used to repeat in class as though driving it home— "you can't accept the gift without The Giver!" What you receive through prayer is a gift from God, but, you must receive, must lay firm hold of, must cleave to the presence of God in the Gift. ■

An Invitation to Study Bible Thursdays, 6:30 pm
mustardseedfaith@bellsouth.net

April 11, 2008

Faith of a mustard seed
by Barbara Woods-Washington, M. Div.

With so little commentary done on **'The Meaning Of The Withered Fig Tree'** who could have known that this 'text led' view of this scripture, (Mark's 5th and final occurrence of 'pistis/faith', 11:20-25) in this small space, would take us into so many dynamics of faith— 'prayer', 'doubt', 'believe', 'receive' — and now 'forgive'!

Barbara Woods Riles Washington

"Whenever you stand praying, forgive, if you have anything against anyone; so that your Father in heaven may also forgive you your trespasses." Mark stands alone in recording this verse as a saying of Jesus' in giving meaning to the withered fig tree. The other 'Double Tradition' Gospel writer, Matthew, records this saying as a part of 'The Sermon on The Mount' (6:14). This reason alone gives cause for New Testament Texual scholars to see problems with this text.

Attention is called again to the fact that several New Testament Greek words lie behind English language translations of 'receive'. With and without textual problems, it must be noted that this study of 'pistis'/faith' usage has and is revealing a consistent journey into the 'saying of Jesus'! All Markan usages of 'aphiemi/forgive' are in the mouth of Jesus!

With the single exception of our present text, all usages of 'aphiemi/forgive' by Jesus in Mark reference 'forgiveness of sin' which was for Him a major theme in His Theology and Ministry. It can easily be thought that this 'dynamic of His faith' is what cost him His life. The examination of Jesus' campaign on 'forgiveness of sins' is of vital importance as we have seen it used several times

☦ 57

"The Voice Of A Proud Community"
Nashville P*R*I*D*E
Pulpit, Pew and Public

already— He said to the paralytic, *"your sins are forgiven."* The response of the scribes on this occasion was *"blasphemy"*— which Jesus, ironically, determines to be the 'unforgivable sin'. When His pronouncements are made concerning 'forgiveness of sins', you can always feel the tension mounting as notes are given of 'counsel being held against Him'.

Here, now, Jesus' final Markan usage of 'pistis/faith' is also His final usage of 'aphiemi/forgive' (vs. 25 & 26). He is downtrodden. His disappointment in humanity has given rise to the 'curing of a tree'! The one follower whom He was developing for the 'church building mission' 'got lost in the tree'! His thoughts, with so little time and so great a salvation yet to be revealed, are as never before. His words come as never before. All in one quick lifetime He has managed to shift forgiveness from being the 'property of the priesthood' to being the responsibility, the obligation, the prayer, the petition of the individual life of faith. Whenever, wherever, whatever you stand praying, forgive anything!!! against anyone!!! Oh my! Oh my... goodness.. and mercy... shall follow me... all the days of my life... How very different this world would be if Christians followed Jesus?■

An Invitation to Study Bible Thursdays, 6:30 pm
mustardseedfaith@bellsouth.net

April 18, 2008

Faith of a mustard seed
by Barbara Woods-Washington, M. Div.

What does Mark say concerning Faith? First the **'Healing Of The Paralytic'**— when four men carrying a paralytic see their 'impossible mission' of getting through this crowd to Jesus. The measure, the measure of faith— removing the roof! Not even for self! *"And when he returned to Caper'na-um after some days, it was reported that he was at home. And many were gathered together, so that there was no longer room for them, not even about the door; and he was preaching the word to them. And they came, bringing to him a paralytic carried by four men. And when they could not get near him because of the crowd, they removed the roof above him; and when they had made an opening, they let down the pallet on which the paralytic lay. And when Jesus saw their faith, he said to the paralytic, "My son, your sins are forgiven." Now some of the scribes were sitting there, questioning in their hearts, "Why does this man speak thus? It is blasphemy! Who can forgive sins but God alone?" And immediately Jesus, perceiving in his spirit that they thus questioned within themselves, said to them, "Why do you question thus in your hearts? Which is easier, to say to the paralytic, 'Your sins are forgiven,' or to say, 'Rise, take up your pallet and walk'? But that you may know that the Son of man has authority on earth to forgive sins" --he said to the paralytic-- "I say to you, rise, take up your pallet and go home."* Jesus saw their faith. The paralytic rose and 'immediately' took up his pallet. The response of those gathered— *"we never saw anything like this!"*

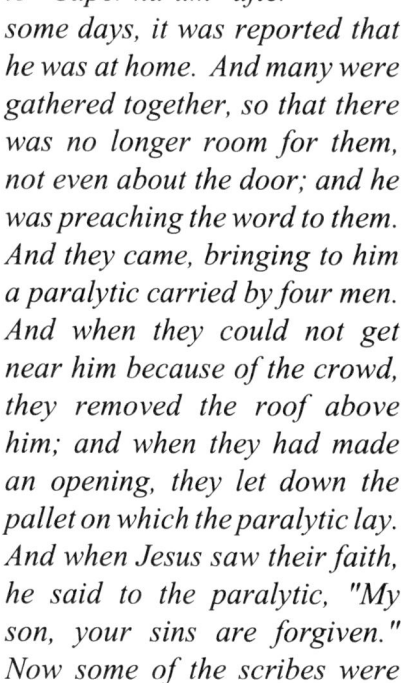

Second, **'The Stilling of The Storm'**— where the

Barbara Woods Riles Washington

"The Voice Of A Proud Community"
Nashville P*R*I*D*E
Pulpit, Pew and Public

✝ 58

disciples woke Jesus saying, *"do you not care if we perish?"* In a 'fresh awakening', Jesus speaks first to nature saying *"Peace. Be still!"* Then he speaks to the Disciples saying, *"Have you no faith?"*

Third, **'A Woman's Faith'**— when Jesus perceiving that power had gone forth from him; says *"daughter, your faith has made you well, go in peace, and be healed of your disease".*

Fourth, **'The Healing of Bartimaeus'**— when, still again, faith and healing are one. Jesus sending followers to call Bartimaeus *"and throwing off his mantle he sprang up and came to Jesus."* Jesus says to Bartimaeus, *"go your way..."*

The 5th and final, **'The Meaning Of The Withered Fig Tree'**— when Peter questions Jesus, *"...the tree which you cursed..."* as it invokes a response of command— *"Have faith in God!".* Prayer, believing, receiving and forgiveness are all used here by Jesus to give meaning to the withered fig tree.

Mark, then, on Faith. All uses of 'pistis/faith' are by Jesus. He sees faith in persons— by what is said and what is done. A 'selfless' magnanimous act: to take the roof off! I recall times when I have been 'so bold' to get to something that 'I wanted', but such brazen boldness for 'someone else's life'? Jesus saw this as faith. For Mark, faith is peace and stillness in the mist of storms. Trusting that Jesus is present and 'He cares', even while sleeping. For Mark, faith is healing; and it's in God! It's praying, believing, receiving and forgiveness.

The foundations are shaking as a result of nature's furry, and in never before places— earthquakes in Illinois and Michigan? Can somebody please wake Jesus up? I'm cursing, fig trees, the president, mortgage lenders, the wars in Iraq and Afghanistan, the (in)justice system, the ever rising price of gasoline, the 'media driven wedge' between Obama and Hillary. This is 'no country for old preachers!' ■

An Invitation to Study Bible Thursdays. 6:30 pm
mustardseedfaith@bellsouth.net

April 25, 2008

Faith of a mustard seed
by Barbara Woods-Washington, M. Div.

I recall the Annual Revivals at St. Stephen's United Church of Christ in Greensboro during my years as Chaplain to Bennett (1988-92). With fond memories I re-live the 'spiritual awakening' we received those weeks as we 'pressed our way' to the Church house 'early enough to get a seat' in what would nightly be a 'shaken together and running over crowd'. Jeremiah Wright was in town! Anyone who has ever experienced the 'very right and reverend' Dr. Jeremiah Wright in the preaching context is very clear about his current 'persecutions' or maybe 'crucifixion?' This calling, as he is currently bold enough to struggle to fulfill, was given in his 'birthright'. I commend to each of you an urgent reading of the Old Testament Book of Jeremiah, lest you be deceived. I give continuous praise, prayer and thanksgiving to God for

Barbara Woods Riles Washington

'this messenger' and very 'rare breed of Man of God'.

Having completed Mark's use of 'pistis/faith', before moving on to Luke, Tillich again, is fruitful as a 'time out'. He writes a message that he entitles— *'Our Ultimate Concern'* for which he takes the text Luke 10:38-42. It too is published in **'The New Being'**.

Mary and Martha, he proposes, become the symbol for two possible attitudes towards life. "Martha is concerned about many things, but all of them are finite, preliminary, transitory. Mary is concerned about one thing, which is infinite, ultimate, lasting."

Concern means involvement. Concern requires a 'part of us in it'. At best concern has 'our heart in it'. Martha's heart was as fully in to 'her distraction' as Mary's heart

✝ 59

'The Voice Of A Proud Community'
Nashville P*R*I*D*E
Pulpit, Pew and Public

was in her 'body bowed listening to Jesus'. Concern is often identified with anxiety. When we become concerned the 'adrenaline flows'. There is even a bit of (self) 'righteous indignation' when 'we be' concerned. "Concern," Tillich states, "provokes compassion or horror."

In the documentary titled **'The Bush Family Fortunes'**, a young black man was interviewed who had been denied voting rights in the presidential election. His name was listed on the notorious **'Florida Convicted Felons List'** that has yet to be reconciled. When asked if he had ever committed a crime he responded, "No. Never. I served in Iraq and have a perfectly clean record". Compassion or horror?

Important to quote, even in length, is this statement. Tillich writes, "Every concern is tyranical and wants our whole heart and our whole mind and our whole strength. Every concern tries to become our ultimate concern, our god. The concern about our work often succeeds in becoming our god, as does the concern about another human being, or about pleasure. The concern about science has succeeded in becoming the god of a whole era in history, the concern about money has become an even more important god, and the concern about the nation the most important god of all."■

An Invitation to Study Bible
Thursdays, 6:30 pm
mustardseedfaith@bellsouth.net

May 2, 2008

Faith of a mustard seed
by Barbara Woods-Washington, M. Div.

Turning now to Luke's use of 'pistis/faith'. Again, as a tool for biblical word usage, I reference <u>Young's Analytical Concordance to the Bible</u>— eleven occurrences

Luke records first the Triple tradition **'The Healing of the Paralytic'** (Luke 5:17-26). Variations include that while Matthew (9:1-8) and Mark (2:1-12) both identify the location of this faith event being at Jesus' home town, no location is given by Luke. His location information is to report that the Pharisees and Scribes present had come from *"every village in Galilee, Judea and Jerusalem"*. Perhaps it is Luke's profession that gave rise to his single tradition statement *"and the power of the Lord was upon him* (Jesus) *to heal"*. We envision a straw or thatched roof in our modern minds but Luke alone records 'tile' being the substance of the roof. To *"let him down with his bed through the tiles"*— not as easy as we think. Where Matthew and Mark both use 'child', Luke uses 'man' and 'you' is added to the pronouncement of 'forgiveness of sins': *"Man, your sins are forgiven you."* The response of those present— *"We have seen strange things today"*.

Barbara Woods Riles Washington

Luke has thus far (in the first four chapters) introduced a Gospel written to he who 'loves God' (Theophilus). The 'Birth Narratives', (of both John The Baptist and Jesus)— 'The Immaculate Conception'; 'Mary's Song'; 'Zachariah's Prophecy' concerning his son; The Shepherds and The Angels; —have given rise to the Christian Church's great 'Silent Night' and 'Peace On Earth' traditions as recounted annually in the Christmas Season. In the

---
✝ 60

"The Voice Of A Proud Community"
Nashville P*R*I*D*E
Pulpit, Pew and Public

first 4 chapters, Luke has told of Jesus' 'Bar Mitzvah'— of Him being 'left in the temple' at the age of 12 unbeknownst to his parents. His 'genealogy'. His 'Wilderness Temptations'. His 'Teaching Ministry'. His 'Trial Sermon' in the Synagogue for which he took the text Isaiah 61— *"The spirit of the Lord is upon me for he has anointed me to bring good news to the poor. He has sent me to proclaim release to the captives and recovery of sight to the blind, to let the oppressed go free, to proclaim the year of the Lord's favor."* His 'Healing Ministry' and spiritual power for 'Exorcism' all in Luke's first 4 chapters.

By the 5th Chapter, His fame had spread far and wide. Not only would a group of men who brought their paralyzed friend on his pallet to be healed by Jesus have a problem getting through the crowd, but, the Pharisees and Scribes, the important men, the learned leaders had come from *"every village in Galilee, Judea and Jerusalem"* to see Him.

It is Luke's 'Healing of the Paralytic' event that introduces 'pistis/faith' and 'controversy'! *"When he saw their faith, he said, Man, your sins are forgiven you."*

Somebody must have called CNN for now, in Luke, His troubles begin. Let's take a closer look.■

An Invitation to Study Bible
Thursdays, 6:30 pm
mustardseedfaith@bellsouth.net

May 9, 2008

Faith of a mustard seed
by Barbara Woods-Washington, M. Div.

'Seeing the faith of the friends' of the paralytic who 'move a tile roof', Luke records Jesus saying to the paralytic, *"Man, your sins are forgiven you."* These words, alone, now cause an immediate change of events. Looking closer, the Pharisees and scribes, who had come from *"every village in Galilee, Judea and Jerusalem"* to see a 'miracle worker', 'healer', 'teacher' now question, *"who is this who is speaking blasphemies?"* (Luke 5:21)

To begin with 'blasphemias' stands alone in translation and can be found in it's original form, even without root variations in most languages. It is used to denote 'abusive speech'; 'word of evil sound'; and came to be known as 'the strongest form of personal mockery and calumniation'. It always refers finally to god. It takes on the sense of 'mistaking the true nature of god'; 'violating god' and 'doubting the power of god'. In the Old Testament it has the sense of 'disputing God's saving power'; 'desecrating His name'. The Rabbis, the scribes and the Pharisees were informed by the Leviticus 24:13ff text: *"He who blasphemes the name of the Lord shall be put to death; all the congregation shall stone him; the sojourner as well as the native, when he blasphemes the Name, shall be put to death".* Israel was even warned of blaspheming the gods of the other nations, lest the foreigner disregard the power of Yahweh. Isaiah recounts Hezekiah's distress as he 'rent his clothes and covered himself with a sack cloth and went into the temple, saying, *"This day is a day of trouble and of blasphemy; children have come to birth, and there is no strength to bring*

Barbara Woods Riles Washington

"The Voice Of A Proud Community"
Nashville P*R*I*D*E
Pulpit, Pew and Public

☦ 61

them forth." When Jesus said to the paralytic, *"Man, your sins are forgiven you",* the scribes and Pharisees asked *"Who is this who is speaking blasphemies?"*

I am reminded of how quickly the Family Reunion, the Family Holiday Dinner and various other purposeful Family gatherings take a change of events. Members are gathered in a kindred spirit of love, fellowship, renewal.. and one person, (drunk or otherwise) will turn it around, upside down.. turn it out! Same person. Every time! (My sister is gon' think I'm talking about her but I haven't named any names! To protect the innocent!).

The Pharisees and scribes, who had come from *"every village in Galilee, Judea and Jerusalem",* surely came the distance to share in a very purposeful gathering of kindred spirits to see, to hear, to be touched by this 'miracle worker', 'healer', 'teacher'. He very simply said to the paralytic, (on a note that was so very personal in Luke— wasn't even talking to THEM), *"Man, your sins are forgiven YOU."* A 'change of events'! A capital crime! Punishable by death! The response of those present— *"We have seen strange things today".* ∎

An Invitation to Study Bible Thursdays. 6:30 pm
mustardseedfaith@bellsouth.net

May 16, 2008

Faith of a mustard seed
by Barbara Woods-Washington, M. Div.

Luke's second use of 'pistis/faith' is a return to **'The Centurion's Servant'** faith event. Matthew's account took two week, initially to explore (Columns of May 25 & June 1, 2007). By December, in my efforts to respond to requests to go further into previous Columns, I arrived here again and wrote:

"Revisiting the discussion on Matthew's 'Centurion's Servant' encounter with Jesus (Matt 8:8ff), I recall now the revelation given in that column— it is the first occurrence in New Testament of both words: 'logos' (word) and 'pistis' (faith). The first time either of these two words are used in scripture is in the mouth of Jesus and used together to experience the centurion in his concern for the illness of 'o pais mou'. (I've added the phrase because in this rare interpretation as servant, the term 'pais' is most always used for child or, here in the masculine, boy or son)."

Barbara Woods Riles Washington

Knowing that I was at a critical text, I put a call in to my only New Testament professor who is still teaching at ITC, Dr. Wayne Merritt (in fact, my New Testament Greek Language professor) in order to be in dialogue with him concerning this text. Being the Christmas season, I left a voice message and passed on by. I want you to know that for 5 months, I have carried this paragraph looking at it from week to week 'knowing' that 'it shall be' dealt with. Now, approaching Luke's version of 'The Centurion's Servant' and his second use of 'pistis/faith'

To begin with, my 'second Bible' is **'The Gospel Parallels'**. It is a Biblical studies tool that I have had since it's required purchase and usage

☦ 62

The Voice Of A Proud Community
Nashville P*R*I*D*E
Pulpit, Pew and Public

in my very first New Testament Literature course. The opening, **'Introduction To Footnote References',** continues to be one of the best concise statements in introducing New Testament Manuscripts to include those written by the Church Fathers and Noncanonical Gospels. I found the original Greek **'Huck'** version at a flee market in Atlanta and have kept the two very close over the years in all my biblical studies work.

Again, today, a peculiarity surrounding this text. 'The Parallels' record a 'double entry' for Luke's version— First, 'The Centurion's Servant' identified as a 'Double Tradition', paralleled with Matthew and silent in Mark; and a second version of the same text 'The Centurion's Slave' identified as a 'Single Tradition', Lucan account!

For those readers of this Column who 'are in the Word', I invite you to read this 'Centurion's Servant' faith event in both records, (Matthew 8:5-13) and Luke 7:1-10 to enter with me into a text that is indeed 'coming alive'.

I am so tempted to sing (I did tell you I was born in the choir?) The song in my head now says, "I serve a risen savior, He's in the world today. I know that He is living, whatever men may say. I see His hand of mercy. I hear His voice of cheer. And just the time I need Him. He's always here. He Lives! He Lives!... "■

An Invitation to Study Bible
Thursdays. 6:30 pm
mustardseedfaith@bellsouth.net

May 23, 2008

Faith of a mustard seed
by Barbara Woods-Washington, M. Div.

"Now a centurion had a slave who was dear to him who was sick and at the point of death." (Luke 7:2). In my small modern slave descendant mind the question arises for me as to why Throckmorton parallel's this text twice with two different titles? First, **'The Centurion's Servant'** paralleled with Matthew; and second, **'The Centurion's Slave'** with no parallel as a Lucan single tradition. Something in 'the cotton' in this very rare translation of 'o pais mou' for a look at the Greek text would definitively suggest the titles 'The Centurion's Son' or 'The Centurion's Boy'.

First a look at the variations. Where Matthew has recorded that the centurion has a personal 'one on one' encounter with Jesus saying, *"my servant is lying paralyzed and in distress"*; Luke's description of the slave's condition is a narrative of a sickness that is 'unto death'. In addition, Luke gives no indication that the centurion ever has a 'face to face' encounter with Jesus. He first sent Elders of the Jews to speak on his behalf and ask Jesus to come and heal his slave. As Jesus approaches the house, the centurion sent friends out to meet him. Whereas the substance of the dialogue is the same— in Matthew, it is directly from the centurion, present and 1st person, or in Luke through the centurion's 'peeps', the Elders and friends, in 3rd person— Jesus see (feels) (knows) unmatchless faith: *"not even in Israel have I found such faith."*

What for most New Testament Theologians would 'not matter' here, 'matters' to me as this text has brought me to a place of critical observation— a 'thorn in my flesh'. The

Barbara Woods Riles Washington

CENTURION'S SLAVE SON (or daughter)! The centurion's servant boy (or girl)!

    I have been doing genealogical research for more than twenty-five years, the results of which I have built the web site www.Magby-SmithFamily.com to resource. With no known interracial marriages in the five generational blood line that I have traced back to Magby slave ownership in Newnan, Coweta County, Georgia, I am still unable to account for the 'whiteness' of my family's skin, with some of my great and great great grand nieces and nephews being born 'white as cotton'? America has asked us 'to forget about' the centurion's (the master) decreeing himself the right to go in and out of our mother's most private life 'depositing seeds' that he would 'own' but never 'give kinship'. Whom he would 'capitalize on' but never 'be familial'.

America wants to 'label', 'rebuke' and 'shun' the 'mad black woman' with no accountability for it's birthing of the 'mad black woman'! Now they say 'get over it'! How do you get over an 'absentee father' who IS A CENTURION? ■

An Invitation to Study Bible Thursdays, 6:30 pm
mustardseedfaith@bellsouth.net

May 30, 2008

Faith of a mustard seed
by Barbara Woods-Washington, M. Div.

"Not even in Israel have I seen such faith!" There was something about this centurion— his attitude? His disposition? His spirit, maybe? His outlook? His humility? His heart, maybe? (I have been told on numerous occasions across the years after proclaiming The Word that "I had touched their heart!" It is so easy for me to tell when 'your heart ain't in it!' I know that it is true— what comes from the heart, reaches the heart!) Perhaps Jesus saw this centurion's heart? But, something about this centurion places him first in the New Testament's model for faith.

"Not even in Israel...". Jesus boldly compares this centurion's faith to the lineage of such a great nation, and so that no mistake is made here, the founding fathers, the patriarchs are named! What is this faith that Jesus saw in just this small encounter with this centurion that he had not seen "even in Israel"?

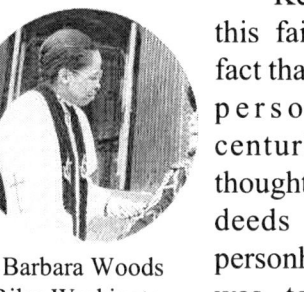

Barbara Woods Riles Washington

Key, for me, in this faith event is the fact that so many of the persons of the centurion station's thoughts, words and deeds towards the personhood of Jesus was to destroy him. Jesus had no money. He had no property. He had no concern for or pursuit of food, clothing or shelter! He had no participation in the national life. He built no house(s) of worship! He himself did not write any testament to his life and ministry. His 'homelessness' was by design! All Jesus had was 'His Word' which as he spoke it to persons of sufferance, they began to follow him around. And yet, he never used the means of those who followed him to alter his 'homeless existence'; which, I think, is a

☦ 64

"The Voice Of A Proud Community"
Nashville P*R*I*D*E
Pulpit, Pew and Public

very vital part of the power of 'His Word'! He never took anything from his followers! To be sure, he charged his disciples to *"take nothing..."*

Jesus had already begun to identify in his 'Word' to the disciples that those of the extreme opposite (the centurion kind) would— (and to be sure did) come to take his life.

Enter a centurion who came taking thought for the wellness of his slave. (Suspect in my small modern mind of course, as a descendent of slaves— he needed him well to continue the servitude.) But Jesus saw something else! *"Not even in Israel have I seen such faith!"* ■

*An Invitation to Study Bible
Thursdays, 6:30 pm
mustardseedfaith@bellsouth.net*

June 6, 2008

Faith of a mustard seed
by Barbara Woods-Washington, M. Div.

Revisiting the 'Experience' component of theology, I turn to the 'Conversion Experience', so very personal in nature that the old spiritual says it best— "You don't know what the Lord told me... You don't know, you wasn't there. You can't say when and you can't say where..."

Barbara Woods
Riles Washington

Notable for word study is the concept 'strepho' which in scripture has the meaning 'to turn'; 'to twist'; 'to bend'; 'to change'. It is used in the Old Testament to refer to inner conversion through suffering or fear. After anointing Saul for the Kingship, he is told by Samuel that the Spirit of the Lord would grip him and he would be changed into another man.

Several forms of 'strepho' are used in scripture, here most notably two: 'apostrepho' (apostacy)— 'to turn away from; 'to turn aside'; 'to turn back'; 'to reject', and 'epistrepho'— 'to turn one's attention to'; 'to pay regard to'; 'to be intentive'; 'to turn one's heart to'; 'to take up a matter'.

Key to the root and most all forms of this word is conscious action. It places this experience time and time again in the very heart of faith as the action relates directly to God. Turning away or turning towards God establishes a relationship that effects how the individual will subsequently experience life and the world in which he lives.

Most recalled in preaching are the conversion experiences of Isaiah and Paul. this single experience of a person's life is spoken of by the worlds greatest theologians as one that so alters, so turns, so twists, so changes the individual's life that 'they will never be the same again!' The 'knowledge/revelation' gained by this experience dictates all future actions on the

The Voice Of A Proud Community
Nashville P*R*I*D*E
Pulpit, Pew and Public

part of the 'changed man'. The world view of the individual is turned towards truth— in seeking, in living and in propagation.

My birth Church used to sing a song that had an amazing level of participation. They sang— "Oh, oh, oh, oh somebody touched me! (3 times) And it must have been the hand of The Lord." Then they sang a verse for each day of the week— "it was on a Monday when somebody touched me! (3 times) And it must have been the hand of The Lord."

Individuals would stand up for the Monday chorus and others would join those standing as each day was called. I remember wondering if and when I was supposed to stand. I knew that whatever they were singing about was so important, so special that each person remembered the very day that it happened to them.

Experiencing God in such a way that your life is 'born again!" New Life! NEW BIRTHDAY! Jesus says that every person MUST have one! ∎

An Invitation to Study Bible Thursdays. 6:30 pm mustardseedfaith@bellsouth.net

June 13, 2008

Faith of a mustard seed
by Barbara Woods-Washington, M. Div.

Just saw a Church Sign which held in public view this statement: 'All new summer Sermons— NO RERUNS!'

Those of you who have been following this 'Faith Of A Mustard Seed' journey may have recognized the 're-runs' of the past five weeks. I have transitioned (again remembering my days of itineracy with the United Methodist Church) from one house to another and am still at the time of this writing 'living out of boxes'. The circumstances of this move is not from 'one Church appointment to another', but beset with a whole new contemporary set of issues that brings a 'new knowledge experience' of the times in which we live.

Jeremiah identified it as a fire that made him 'weary with holding it in'. Suffice it to say that the words of the gospel choir's song has new meaning— '...but in every situation, God gives consolation, that trials come to only make us strong!Through it all... I've learned to trust in Jesus. I've learned to trust in God.' And so remaining true to the task of this column, what Faith statement can be made?

Barbara Woods Riles Washington

Tillich's definition of faith continues to provide the foundation— FAITH IS ULTIMATE CONCERN! At this point we must raise the question of what we are concerned about? It is a very simple and elementary formula in our times— M + E = ME! If it is not happening to me, 'I am' unconcerned! If 'I am' not (visibly) affected, it is not my concern! As long as it does not knock on (down) my door, I won't get involved.

I went into the convenient store at 28th and Jefferson Street,

✝ 69

"The Voice Of A Proud Community"
Nashville P*R*I*D*E
Pulpit, Pew and Public

the only store so far as I can see, in my new community. I immediately took note of the foreign proprietorship and began to wonder how a single store of this kind would come to service the entire University and surrounding community. By the time I tried to select items for purchase I took note of the cost! I paid for a single drink and was 'no longer holding it in' as I verbalized my distrust in their taking advantage of a 'student population'!... all the way out the door!

Now ME, I have been driving the distance to return to communities where the 'excessive mark-up' is not being felt and where 'quality', 'choice' and 'service' factor into cost. So it is not happening to me, 'I am' unconcerned??? 'I am' not (visibly) affected, it is not my concern??? It is not knocking (on) down my door, I won't get involved???

I keep hearing Jesus' Call To Self-Denial— "if any one would come after me, let him deny himself...!" Ultimate Concern.■

An Invitation to Study Bible Thursdays, 6:30 pm
mustardseedfaith@bellsouth.net

July 11, 2008

Faith of a mustard seed
by Barbara Woods-Washington, M. Div.

Luke's third use of 'pistis/faith' has been used by the world's greatest preachers as a life message with numerous lessons. As a part of Lectionary Studies, it has been used across the years by the Church to teach perhaps the Gospel's greatest example of forgiveness of sin. Feminist Theologians have written commentary on this text to examine this woman's place in the ministry of the Church. Gospel music artists have 'sung' this woman's place into the hearts of Christendom. It is a passage of scripture so poetic in content that **'A Sinful Woman Forgiven'** requires a reading of the text in it's entirety. Hear now the Word of The Lord from Luke 7:36-50:

Barbara Woods Riles Washington

"One of the Pharisees asked Jesus to eat with him, and he went into the Pharisee's house and took his place at the table. And a woman in the city, who was a sinner, having learned that he was eating in the Pharisee's house, brought an alabaster jar of ointment. She stood behind him at his feet, weeping, and began to bathe his feet with her tears and to dry them with her hair. Then she continued kissing his feet and anointing them with the ointment. Now when the Pharisee who had invited him saw it, he said to himself, 'If this man were a prophet, he would have known who and what kind of woman this is who is touching him—that she is a sinner.' Jesus spoke up and said to him, 'Simon, I have something to say to you.' 'Teacher,' he replied, 'speak.' 'A certain creditor had two debtors; one owed five hundred denarii, and the other fifty. When they could not pay, he cancelled the debts for both of them. Now which of them will love him more?' Simon

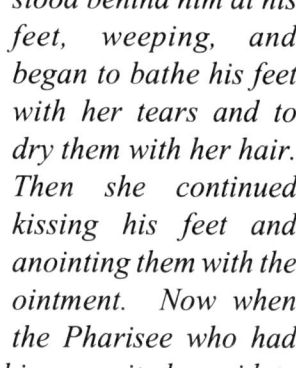

"The Voice Of A Proud Community"
Nashville P*R*I*D*E
Pulpit, Pew and Public

☦ 70

answered, 'I suppose the one for whom he cancelled the greater debt.' And Jesus said to him, 'You have judged rightly.' Then turning towards the woman, he said to Simon, 'Do you see this woman? I entered your house; you gave me no water for my feet, but she has bathed my feet with her tears and dried them with her hair. You gave me no kiss, but from the time I came in she has not stopped kissing my feet. You did not anoint my head with oil, but she has anointed my feet with ointment. Therefore, I tell you, her sins, which were many, have been forgiven; hence she has shown great love. But the one to whom little is forgiven, loves little.' Then he said to her, 'Your sins are forgiven.' But those who were at the table with him began to say among themselves, 'Who is this who even forgives sins?' And he said to the woman, 'Your faith has saved you; go in peace."

CeCe sings it this way: "The room grew still as she made her way to Jesus. She stumbles through the tears that made her blind. She felt such pain, some spoke in anger. Heard folks whisper, 'there's no place here for her kind.' Still on she came, through the shame that flushed her face until at last she knelt before His feet. And though she spoke no words, everything she said was heard. As she poured her love for the Master from her box of Alabaster. I've come to pour my praise on Him like oil from Mary's Alabaster Box. Don't be angry if I wash His feet with my tears and I dry them with my hair. You weren't there the night He found me. You did not feel what I felt when He wrapped His love all around me. And, you don't know the cost of the oil..." ■

An Invitation to Study Bible Thursdays. 6:30 pm mustardseedfaith@bellsouth.net

---

July 18, 2008

Faith of a mustard seed
by Barbara Woods-Washington, M. Div.

"And a woman in the city, who was a sinner, having learned that he was eating at the Pharisee's house, brought an alabaster jar of ointment."

Kittel's Theological Dictionary of The New Testament, finds it necessary to examine separate and apart from the word 'amartia/sin', the term 'amartolos/sinner' as an adjective. Having defined sin as 'a power hostile to God'— sinner now becomes a value judgement from the human standpoint. Although much speculation about her background and character has been projected, it is **'A Sinful Woman Forgiven'** who is the 3rd 'pistis/faith' revelation in Luke's Gospel.

There are only 3 known instances of the word 'amartolos/sinner' in Classical Greek. For Aristotle, his only use of sinner is in reference to "slaves of bad character".

Barbara Woods Riles Washington

Again, in Lycaonian inscriptions from Imperial Rome, it is used in 'curses on the violators of graves'. I am reminded of the historical plundering of the Pharoah's tombs, yet knowing the wealth stored in those graves I can readily see how this grave robber can be judged a sinner. For the Stoics, it is not derogatory in use but of a man's 'stumbling from one failing to another' perhaps into worthlessness. We have all often wondered about the family member or friend or acquaintance who seems to have this curse— 'can't do nothing right'!

New Testament use of 'amartolos/sinner' is clearly defined by it's Old Testament meaning and usage. 94 uses of 'sinner' in the OT— 68 of which are found in the Psalter alone. A clear picture of 'the sinner',

"The Voice Of A Proud Community"
Nashville P*R*I*D*E
Pulpit, Pew and Public

then, can be ascertained from the Psalmist. He is the opposite of the 'pious, righteous and godly'. He breaks the commandments and trust in his own power and wealth and understanding. There is often a complete dismissal of God in his life. As 'The Law—Torah' becomes the 'center of life' for the OT believer, the study of and devotion to Torah is what 'keeps from sin'. So important to the Psalmist is this understanding, that the very FIRST PSALM opens this wisdom book by saying: *"Blessed is the man that walks not in the counsel of the ungodly, nor stands in the way of sinners... But his delight is in The Law of The Lord and in this law does he meditate, DAY and NIGHT!"*

It is no small thing that 'this woman who was a sinner' dared to enter the house of a Pharisee! Had she been to the synagogue? Probably not. Had she been studying and meditating on the Law day and night? I think that would be a no. Was she pious? Righteous? Godly? Could never be in this house— a woman? In this environment, she was indeed worthless. She did not know Torah... she knew nothing— all based upon a value judgement from the human (Pharisaic) standpoint! She knew this— I am looking for Jesus. I want to anoint him with my alabaster jar of ointment! ■

An Invitation to Study Bible Thursdays, 6:30 pm mustardseedfaith@bellsouth.net

July 25, 2008

Faith of a mustard seed
by Barbara Woods-Washington, M. Div.

"She stood behind him at his feet, weeping, and began to bathe his feet with her tears and to dry them with her hair. Then she continued kissing his feet and anointing them with the ointment." Luke 7:38

Noteworthy is this act of 'kissing his feet'— a thought that would never cross the mind of modern man. The thought of which for the modern child would bring great disgust— I've already seen 'the head bobbin' and the 'the hand motion' to the saying "I ain't kissing nobody's— feet!"

The word rendered 'kissing' here in this text is 'katephilei' a rarely used form of philos — (philosophy; Philadelphia). No better time to enter a discussion on the use of 'love' in the New Testament. For the sake of a new level of understanding, we are reminded by Kittel that there is no use of 'eros' (erotic love) in NT. The separation of 'eros' from 'philos' (both of which the English language translates into a single word 'love') is, I believe, a critical point for dialogue in all Biblical Studies. It would improve human relationships greatly— for "What the world needs now is (STILL) Love", but PHILOS— untangled from the multi trillion dollar 'eros' industry. While visiting a former parishioner hospitalized in Atlanta this past week-end, I learned of a family friend who had been molesting his granddaughter. When his acts were discovered he ended his life with a gunshot to his head.

'Philos/love', then, is 'to regard and treat somebody as one of one's own people'; 'natural attraction to those who belong'; 'love for close relatives'. It is used for the love a parents to the child; and shifts from 'that which belongs to that

Barbara Woods Riles Washington

✝ 72

"The Voice Of A Proud Community"
Nashville P*R*I*D*E
Pulpit, Pew and Public

which is chosen.' 'The love of friends'. As when you hear persons who have strong marriages say "we were friends before we were lovers." In it's earliest usage 'katephilei/kissing' is found only in reference to close relatives. Children are kissed by parents— an act of love so very personal that it is thought that 'this transfer of breath', the soul, inward 'living fellowship' is being set up for eternity. (The umbilical cord could never be broken!) Then, later for rulers as the element of respect and honor are added to love in the kiss. From the face to the hand to the feet as it becomes an act of homage. Subjects 'bowed down prostrate' to show love for kings and later in the Church to greet Popes. In this prostrate position subjects began to 'kiss the feet' to honor rulers.

It has been said that *"there is no greater love than a man would lay down his life for a friend."* That this woman, judged a sinner, (labeled and thought of as 'worthless'), could enter this hostile environment, (where the 'back biting' was being poured out in her hearing), and complete her mission— IS A GREATer LOVE! Her act of faith is seen by the Master and merits her a place in Biblical History with a pronouncement of peace— beyond measure!■

*An Invitation to Study Bible
Thursdays, 6:30 pm
mustardseedfaith@bellsouth.net*

August 1, 2008

Faith of a mustard seed
by Barbara Woods-Washington, M. Div.

"Now when the Pharisee who had invited him saw it, he said to himself, 'If this man were a prophet, he would have known who and what kind of woman this is who is touching him—that she is a sinner'." (Luke 7:39)

In spite of the continued debate concerning the authenticity of the 'Willie Lynch Speech of 1712 Virginia', I am convinced of the psychological substance as it relates to 'mind control' in the making of a slave. "I guarantee every one of you that if installed correctly it will control the slaves for at least 300 years. ...take the differences and make them bigger... age; gender; color— pit the dark skinned slave against the light skinned; ...use fear, distrust and envy for control... if used intensely for one year the slaves themselves will remain perpetually distrustful."

Barbara Woods Riles Washington

Take note of (Simon) the Pharisee who had invited Him, 'thinking out loud— talking to himself!' Seeing this woman 'kissing the feet of Jesus' and 'anointing Him with her costly oil', he said to himself, *'If this man were a prophet, he would have known who and what kind of woman this is who is touching him—that she is a sinner'.*

I am reminded of my sorority days while a student at Tennessee State University, those years of 'color blindness'. Intense initiation! There was an exercise where a Big Sister would point to any color and ask 'what color is this? The pledges' response is the same color every time. The organization's color is 'all you see'! Those years when 'saying to one's self'— (in fear, distrust and envy; 'hating') that persons wearing other colors are 'not to

✝ 73

"The Voice Of A Proud Community"
Nashville P*R*I*D*E
Pulpit, Pew and Public

be trusted!' Not to mention the threats of violence. And to see how it has manifested itself among our younger generations— too, 'wearing colors'. No longer the need for death and destruction to come from 'without', it now comes from 'within'.

Don't get it twisted. As a College Chaplain I continue to think and recommend the sorority and fraternity to 'every person' who receives the gift of this level of education. I also say to them it doesn't matter what you pledge, one is not greater than the other. Me, I look forward to the day that the 'differences made bigger in the mind of the slave' might be as 'the high places— they shall come down'. I've been to the mountain top and see the AKAs and Deltas join hands in Washington, DC and "sing that old Negro spiritual... Free at last! Free at last! Thank God almighty..." The day that these two organizations get together 'in being about the business of freeing our people'— we will be free... indeed!

Simon had a 'difference made bigger' in his mind— he, a Pharisee and she, a sinner. He talked to himself, he said to himself that if Jesus were a prophet... He would already know... ■

An Invitation to Study Bible Thursdays. 6:30 pm mustardseedfaith@bellsouth.net

August 8, 2008

Faith of a mustard seed
by Barbara Woods-Washington, M. Div.

"Then turning towards the woman, he said to Simon, 'Do you see this woman? I entered your house; you gave me no water for my feet, but she has bathed my feet with her tears and dried them with her hair. You gave me no kiss, but from the time I came in she has not stopped kissing my feet. You did not anoint my head with oil, but she has anointed my feet with ointment. Therefore, I tell you, her sins, which were many, have been forgiven; hence she has shown great love. But the one to whom little is forgiven, loves little." (Luke 7:44-47)

Barbara Woods Riles Washington

I have given a lot of thought to just how it is that this woman could be judged so great a sinner, as many other women in the Biblical narrative have been. With so little power over the smallest events of her times, what could she have possibly done to be labeled— and known by so many as 'a sinner'?

Having come out of a statistic of up to 70% of the families being headed up by women— generations of 'no father' influences in children's lives, I know many a woman who 'did what she had to do' in order to feed, clothe, and shelter her children. In a world that would show her 'eros/love', but never 'philos/love'— and then judge her 'a sinner'.

I recall a day in my days of student ministry while in Seminary in Atlanta. I was at Grady Hospital on a sick visit and found myself sitting in the waiting room opposite two men from Ebenezer Baptist Church also there waiting to call upon sick members. They were upward in age and though casual in dress, both had on their left chest what I thought to be ' a sheriff's badge', but upon closer look it read 'Deacon'. Even

☦ 74

'The Voice Of A Proud Community'
Nashville P*R*I*D*E
Pulpit, Pew and Public

with this level of 'authority', most memorable was the heavy set man with his cane held tightly in his hand as he, even while sitting, leaned upon it. As they talked about their purpose, I said to them that I too, am a Deacon, having received my first ordination in the United Methodist Church. They looked at each other with a face of having 'smelled something— bad'! Then the one with the cane began to beat it upon the floor as he said to me, "God ain't called no woman to preach!" This image is one that I shall never forget—as though they could 'beat me' into believing that my calling is not sure. My immediate response was an outburst of laughter. Their expressions of disgust turned into a look of hatred and I said "no, no, I'm not laughing at you, it's just that the way that God is already using me, it's funny to me that you can't know!"

Jesus asked *Simon "Do you see this woman?"* Look again at the clear picture of 'the sinner' ascertained from the Psalmist. He is the opposite of the 'pious, righteous and godly'. (She is sick and tired of his piousness, righteousness and godliness). He breaks the commandments and trust in his own power and wealth and understanding. (Her lack of power and lack of wealth and mis-understanding is sometimes all that she has). There is often a complete dismissal of God in his life. (Many nights as she cries about how she is being treated and how she will feed her children she wonders 'where is God'?)

As 'The Law—Torah' becomes the 'center of life' for the Old Testament believer, the study of and devotion to Torah is what 'keeps from sin'. Jesus asked Simon "Do you see this woman?" I see now. As long as women allow a male dominated system— (theologically, socially, economically, etc.), to keep us from preaching— we remain 'a sinner'!■

An Invitation to Study Bible Thursdays, 6:30 pm mustardseedfaith@bellsouth.net

---
August 15, 2008

Faith of a mustard seed
by Barbara Woods-Washington, M. Div.

"But those who were at the table with him began to say among themselves, 'Who is this who even forgives sins?'" (Luke 7:49)

This is not the first time in Luke's Gospel that controversy has arisen concerning Jesus' pronouncement of 'the forgiveness of sin'. This, Luke's 3rd use of 'pistis/faith'— **'A Sinful Woman Forgiven'** is now directly linked to his 1st use of 'pistis/faith'— the 'Healing of the Paralytic'. (Luke 5:17-26)

A closer look reveals that Jesus sees faith in the friends of a paralytic who remove a roof to get into the house to see Jesus. There is no foreknowledge, no whispering, no judgement, no indication of sin in the life of this man. He came for 'healing'— yet, Jesus pronounced *"your sins are forgiven"!* Jesus, then, sees faith in a woman who comes alone to get into the house to see Him. There is foreknowledge, whispering, judgement, and perhaps a 'casting the first stone' indication of sin in the life of this woman. Since there is no apparent sickness or disease in her life, it is only in believing that one can 'get her purpose'— yet, Jesus gives the same pronouncement *"your sins are forgiven"!*

Barbara Woods Riles Washington

Earliest use of 'aphiemi/forgiveness' has the sense of 'to send off'; 'to hurl'; 'to release'; 'to abandon'; to surrender'; and can be seen in the Greek legal system in release from a legal relation: 'to release from debt'; 'to release from punishment'. The object may be material or personal but is never religious.

Old Testament as a legalistic faith, sees this as a legal relationship between man and God— but now the object is GOD ALONE! Taking on the sense of 'remission' where the

☦ 75

"The Voice Of A Proud Community"
Nashville P*R*I*D*E
Pulpit, Pew and Public

object of remission is sin or guilt. Then it becomes cultic— where the 'removal of sin' the 'expiation of sin' is only done by ritual. *"Who, but God,* (through the High Priest in the Holy of Holies) *can forgive sin?"*

Jesus, all up in the midst of a belief that only God; only the High Priest can pronounce 'forgiveness of sin'— comes telling a paralytic, his friends and all those gathered in this house, (who have sin as the furthest thing from their judgment)— *"your sins are forgiven"!* Jesus, all up in another house full of believers (who have sin as the only thing in their judgment)— comes telling a woman the exact same thing, *"your sins are forgiven"!*

This release from debt; this release from punishment; the send off, abandon, surrender; remission, expiation is done for ALL, EVERY ONE— as Jesus takes His Old Testament faith to another level. Whether it was the (fully) God nature or the (fully) Man nature in him that gave him the authority to forgive sins, I don't know. All they wanted to know was ... *who is this?* ■

An Invitation to Study Bible Thursdays. 6:30 pm
mustardseedfaith@bellsouth.net

August 22, 2008

Faith of a mustard seed
by Barbara Woods-Washington, M. Div.

"And he said to the woman, 'Your faith has saved you; go in peace." (Luke 7:50)

Soteriology, the word, the study of salvation is the ultimate concern of the religious life. To be sure, the question was put to Jesus by a rich young ruler asking *"what must I do to be saved?"* Jesus required of him to sell what he had and give to the poor. In his going away sorrowful, the disciples ask, *"then who can be saved?"*

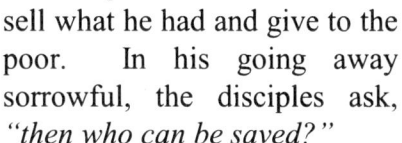

'Sozo', the word in which 'saved' of this text finds root has the sense of— 'To make safe, sound'; 'to deliver from a direct threat'; 'to bring safe and sound out of a difficult situation'; 'preserving the inner being'; 'deliverance from condemnation'.

In case you missed it, Jesus is now taking 'pistis/faith' to a whole other level. There has previously been a concentration on faith as 'healing action'.

Barbara Woods Riles Washington

Jesus has taught those who drew near to him in faith who were in need of healing from infirmities, from diseases, from sickness— even unto death, that 'faith heals'. He has used faith where he found it in believers to bring forgiveness of sins directly to us, notwithstanding a traditional ritualistic ownership. Now Jesus is saying to the woman that her faith makes her safe and sound! Her faith delivers her from direct threat. Faith brings safe and sound out of a difficult situation. Faith will preserve the inner being. Faith gives deliverance from condemnation.

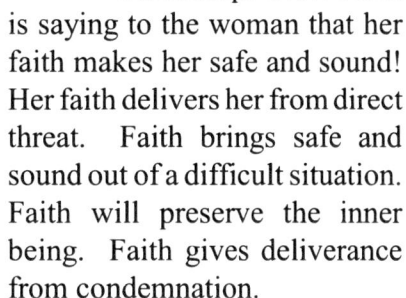

I am reminded of my interview with the Pastor-Parish Relations Committee at the Gladstone-Peapeck Church in New Jersey during my year of Doctoral Biblical Studies at Drew. I had been forewarned by the District Superintendent that

"The Voice Of A Proud Community"
Nashville P*R*I*D*E
Pulpit, Pew and Public

not only was this an all white congregation, but only one black family lived in this town. I received an invitation from a young couple, (the husband of which was on the committee), to have dinner in their home and that he would take me to the Church. They warned me of the woman who was to be my biggest adversary. During the meeting I knew exactly who she was by the look on her face— 'smelled something'? By the time she spoke she said that music is different in the White Church from in the Black Church traditions. She questioned how I would handle the difference in church music. I said to her that music was the least of my concerns. I understand that I would be the 3rd woman that this Church has had as pastor. "I think you'll need a man!" The outburst of laughter was one of the most liberating moments I have experienced in my life. Everything changed in the moment. The DS called the next day to say that he was not expecting the outcome of the meeting. There was a unanimous vote that I should come to serve as their Pastor.

This woman, who biblical history has come to label 'A Sinful Woman' has now found a place in Soteriological History! She has made salvation history! Her act of faith has been recounted by Jesus as he asks *"Simon, do you see this woman?"*

Her 'inner being is preserved' when Jesus said her... *"go in peace!"* ∎

An Invitation to Study Bible Thursdays, 6:30 pm mustardseedfaith@bellsouth.net

August 29, 2008

Faith of a mustard seed
by Barbara Woods-Washington, M. Div.

"And he said to the woman, 'Your faith has saved you; go in peace." (Luke 7:50)

How fitting a place to leave the discussion on the **'A Sinful Woman Forgiven'**, Luke's third use of 'pistis/faith', at the point of Jesus giving her peace, even in the midst of the abuse from Simon as an unwelcome visitor in his house. No simple thing, for it is the same peace that Jesus leaves the world as he ascends in resurrection... a brand new life of peace.

Jesus wept in John's Gospel when he saw the distress of Mary who threw herself at his feet weeping saying *'Lord if you had been here my brother* (Lazarus) *would not have died'*. During our childhood Vacation Bible School days we learned it to be the shortest verse of scripture and some, like my brother, when the tradition of going around the table and saying a Bible verse before the meal was practiced, always just said, *"Jesus wept."*

Barbara Woods Riles Washington

But it is Jesus' weeping in Luke's Gospel that has a more far reaching significance. It was on the day that the Church has come to know as Palm Sunday. The 'Triumphant Entry' into the city riding on a colt. As he came near and saw the city, he wept saying, *"Would that even today you knew the things that make for peace!"* And he began to prophesy.

The discussion of the Old Testament Hebrew—'shalom' would take a whole other study, so in this small space we look at 'eirene' as used by Jesus in this text. A basic feature of this word is that it rarely denotes relationship. It's not an attitude, but a state of being. It is extolled by Philemon in classical Greek as a 'supreme good'. It is 'a state' from which flows all blessings for both land and people. Epictetus thinks it to be the 'absence of hostility'. While the Stoics sense it to be 'a desired state of mind'. There is a predominance of it's usage in 'the greeting' in New Testament with the sense of 'well being'.

For Paul, peace is primary. It is his salutation as he greets both Jew and Gentile. He understands it to be from God as he not only comes into presence speaking peace, but it is also, as with Jesus, his benediction, *"and the peace of God which passes all understanding, will keep your hearts and mind in Christ Jesus."*

The principle meaning of 'eirene' in NT is 'salvation', particularly when used by Jesus— peace as a state of reconciliation with God. *"Let not your hearts be troubled... Peace I leave with you; My peace I give to you; not as the world gives..."*

Jesus grieves, then, over our inability to see the things that make for peace. Simon knew nothing about peace on this day, let alone peace being found in his home. After explaining a few things to Simon about the *'the things that make for peace'*, Jesus said to the woman, 'you go girl! You go in peace!' ∎

An Invitation to Study Bible Thursdays. 6:30 pm mustardseedfaith@bellsouth.net

September 5, 2008

Faith of a mustard seed
by Barbara Woods-Washington, M. Div.

Luke's fourth use of 'pistis/faith' is the triple tradition **'The Calming Of The Storm'** (Luke 8:22-25). All three recordings of this pericope are close in detail. Significant is two dialogical variations: First, in what the disciples say upon waking Jesus and second, what Jesus says in response. Matthew records the disciples saying, *"Save, Lord; we are perishing."* (Matt 8:23-27). Mark records this as a question, *"Teacher, do you not care if we perish?"* (Mark 4:35-41). Where Luke records their saying *"Master, Master, we are perishing!"* Jesus' response for all three Gospel writers is in the form of a question: *"Why are you afraid, O men of little faith?"* (Matthew); *"Why are you afraid? Have you no faith?"* (Mark); and *"Where is your faith?"* (Luke)

Luke stands alone in ascribing 'danger' to the sea's storm that has risen in this text. To be sure, all indications are given that the very nature of this storm was so great that the water had already begun to fill the boat. But the use of 'ekindunenon/danger' here by Luke is so rare that the word is not identified in Young's in it's Luke occurrence and the only use, one single use given is in Act 19. Even more unusual is Kittel's 10 Volume work has total omission of this word 'ekindunenon/danger' while it discusses 'enoxos' the danger of judgement spoken of in Matthew and the danger of eternal damnation spoken of in Mark.

I can't help but think about the great storms that have presently become such a phenomenal part of our life and times. So much has been said in the aftermath of Katrina that, I believe the images to be worth a

Barbara Woods Riles Washington

"The Voice Of A Proud Community"
Nashville P*R*I*D*E
Pulpit, Pew and Public

† 78

thousand words in speaking historically about this 'ekindunenon/danger'. Outstanding in my mind is the image of the Crescent City Connection bridge where evacuees were met by the shotguns of the Gretna Police Department. Those chosen and commissioned 'to protect and to serve' used the violent forces of (hu)man(ity) to intensify the 'ekindunenon/danger'. In the 'fear for life' that is inherent in the 'ekindunenon/danger' of the sea's storm, I can only imagine in my mind's eye the fear of those persons standing on that bridge as they heard gunshots— from police!

The experience of 'ekindunenon/danger' has challenged the very moral fiber of this nation. Arthur, Bertha, Christobal, Dolly, Edouard, Fay, Gustav, Hanna, and Ike are only 9 of the 21 Atlantic storms identified in 2008. In preparation for this 'ekindunenon/danger', thousands of residents of Louisiana have again been displaced, even as we speak, in Tennessee, Florida, Texas but I continue to wonder how many are, this time, in Gretna? The other danger, 'enoxos' kicks in— 'will you be ready (when He comes?).

The disciples fear was so great in the midst of this storm of the sea, this 'ekindunenon/danger', that they repeated their call out to the Lord— *"Master, Master..."* And the response is still the same... *"Where Is Your Faith?"*

Those of us who are 'ole school' gospel music lovers, hold high on the list James Cleveland's interpretation of this text. I still have the need to hear him sing— 'Master, the tempest is raging. The billows are tossing high. The sky is all shadowed with blackness. No shelter on earth is nigh. Carest Thou not that we perish? O how can Thy lie asleep? It seems like each moment so madly is threatening. A grave in the angry deep. Get up Jesus...' ■

An Invitation to Study Bible Thursdays, 6:30 pm mustardseedfaith@bellsouth.net

September 12, 2008

Faith of a mustard seed
by Barbara Woods-Washington, M. Div.

"And when the woman saw that she was not hidden, she came trembling, and falling down before him declared in the presence of all the people why she had touched him, and how she had been immediately healed." (Luke 8:47)

Luke's fifth use of 'pistis/faith' is a triple tradition that has already been viewed in Matthew and Mark. It is **'A Woman's Faith'** which, again, sits in the middle of Jesus' call to go and see about Jairus' daughter. Variations include Luke's statement that *"she could not be healed by anyone"* (Luke 8:43-48); while Matthew is silent on her medical history (Matthew 9:20-22); and Mark speaks of her suffering under physicians and the draining of her resources while seeking healing (Mark 5:25-34). For Mark, the disciples question why he would even ask *"who touched me"*; while for Luke, when all denied, Peter says, *"Master... it's the multitudes!"* And then Luke alone records that *"when the woman saw that she was not hidden..."*.

Barbara Woods Riles Washington

So very difficult is this concept of 'hidden', as so many words are used biblically to give meaning. In all true religions there is 'mystery of the Divine' that is hidden. To be sure, Jesus adopted a teaching method of using 'parables', indicating that keys to the Kingdom of Heaven would remain hidden from plain sight. Some would see, but not see; some would hear but not understand. In Luke, Jesus attributes this 'hiddenness' to the will of God as he prayed *"I thank you Father, Lord of heaven and earth, because you have hidden these things from the wise and intelligent and have revealed them to infants; yes,*

✝ 79

"The Voice Of A Proud Community"
Nashville P*R*I*D*E
Pulpit, Pew and Public

Father, for such was your gracious will" (10:21). It is only by 'revelation' that the 'Mysterium Tremendium' becomes known by the believer.

I can't help but recall the late Dr. Isaac Clark's Homiletics classroom when he talked about 'revelation coming through the preached word'. An original stand-up commedian, he would say "Do you see the lightening flashing? Crackity, crack, crack, crack. Can you hear the thunder rolling? Boomity, bam, bam, bam!"

When 'hidden' relates to (hu)man, it has within it not just the sense of 'to cover'; 'to conceal'; but the sense of 'to deceive' is introduced to the concept. Adam hid from God when the knowledge of good and evil came into his life. There is also the sense 'to be ashamed' now experienced in the concept of 'hidden'. With two on-going wars; seven million foreclosed homes (a never before seen 'homeless' America); a stock market crash; etc, much of what has been hidden MUST COME to light!

Even with her matchless faith which gave her 'heart' to go up and touch Jesus to receive her healing, this woman was 'covered' by the crowd which enabled her to 'think' that she was 'hidden' from Jesus. Ashamed at not speaking up when he asked, it was not until 'He saw her' that she came forth trembling..." ■

An Invitation to Study Bible Thursdays, 6:30 pm mustardseedfaith@bellsouth.net

September 19, 2008

Faith of a mustard seed
by Barbara Woods-Washington, M. Div.

"Jesus said to his disciples, "Occasions for stumbling are bound to come, but woe to anyone by whom they come! It would be better for you if a millstone were hung around your neck and you were thrown into the sea than for you to cause one of these little ones to stumble. Be on your guard! If another disciple sins, you must rebuke the offender, and if there is repentance, you must forgive. And if the same person sins against you seven times a day, and turns back to you seven times and says, 'I repent,' you must forgive." The apostles said to the Lord, "Increase our faith!". (Luke 17:1-5)

Immediately following, what I think to be one of the most powerful parables of the Gospel, Luke's single tradition telling of *'The Rich Man and Lazarus'*— is Luke's sixth use of 'pistis/faith'. It is a conglomeration of both a triple

Barbara Woods
Riles Washington

tradition, **'On Causing Sin'** and a double tradition, **'On Forgiveness'** that have not been previously viewed in that Luke stood alone in recording the petition, *"Increase our faith!"*

Jesus has told of a rich man who, while tormented by the flames of hell has a change of heart— If Lazarus could be sent to his father's house to warn his five brothers they would repent. Father Abraham, Jesus says, told the rich man, *"if they listen not to Moses and the prophets, they will not be convinced even if someone rises from the dead"*. While 'the parable' is most always used in public hearing, here the chapter breaks to indicate that we have now entered a private hearing for the benefit of his disciples. I found these teachings so masterful that I chose "The Parables with

"The Voice Of A Proud Community"
Nashville P*R*I*D*E
Pulpit, Pew and Public

Private Interpretation In Mark" as my area of dissertation research while matriculating in the New Testament Biblical Studies Doctoral program at Drew University. In 'private interpretation' (identified in Mark as 'keys to the Kingdom') on the meaning of 'The Rich Man and Lazarus' parable, Jesus speaks to the disciples 'On Causing Sin' and 'On Forgiveness'.

'Skandala' is the term used here of which Jesus warns of a retribution 'worse than death' for the offender. One sure indication of the difficulty in understanding is when so many translations use a different word— (KJV) offenses; (RSV) sin; (NRSV) stumbling; (NJB) falling, etc.; while the word itself translates 'scandal'. A peculiar etymology in how far 'skandala' has come from it's original Greek usage. It's biblical usage is controlled by the theology of Judaism and is absent from Greek thought and literature. Noteworthy is Kittel's discussion on this word written by Stahlin, "What is at issue in 'skandalon' is the relation to God. The skandalon is an obstacle in coming to faith and a cause of going astray in it. As in OT it is the cause of both transgression and destruction, for a fall in faith is a fall in the absolute sense."

You will (passively) 'skandalon/scandal', offend, sin, stumble, fall, but— to be the cause (actively) of skandalon carries with it a fate; for— *"It would be better for you if a millstone were hung around your neck and you were thrown into the sea".*■

*An Invitation to Study Bible Thursdays, 6:30 pm
mustardseedfaith@bellsouth.net*

September 26, 2008

Faith of a mustard seed
by Barbara Woods-Washington, M. Div.

"Take heed to yourselves. If your brother sins, rebuke him, and if he repents, forgive him. If he sins against you seven times in a day, and seven times comes back to you and says, 'I repent,' forgive him." The apostles said to the Lord, "Increase our faith!." (Luke 17:3-5)

In this, Luke's sixth use of 'pistis/faith' pericope, is a double tradition teaching of Jesus **'On Forgiveness'**. The variations are so noteworthy that the verses are contextually different for Matthew. Verse 3, for Matthew, speaks of telling your brother of his fault between you and him alone. If he listens, Jesus says in Matthew, *"you have gained your brother"*. Verse 4, Matthew records as a question asked by Peter, *"Lord, How often shall my brother sin against me and I forgive him?"* To which Jesus replies, *"Seventy times seven."*

Luke alone records Jesus' teachings 'On Forgiveness' as a

Barbara Woods Riles Washington

'formula': SIN—REBUKE; REPENT—FORGIVE. If we have not gotten the critical nature of these 'final four' terms as they weight heavily in any religious life, Luke precedes this with the warning, 'prosexete/take heed, be on guard'!

The Biblical history of 'amartano/sin' is one that merits full disclosure. To be sure, from the Genesis account of 'The Fall', throughout the coming of The Messiah— ALL is done by God to rescue (hu)man(ity) from sin and death. For the Gospel writers, Jesus IS VICTORIOUS! We have previously looked at His controversial work in the areas of SIN—FORGIVEness (which would get him killed!). Now, Luke calls attention to 'epitimeson/Rebuke' as reaction to sin by a brother, and 'metanoese/Repentance' as a

"The Voice Of A Proud Community"
Nashville P*R*I*D*E
Pulpit, Pew and Public

prerequisite to Forgiveness. What a difficult task is given the Christian disciple here in first being 'so on guard' against sin in our own lives that we are able to point to sin, no, 'rebuke' sin in our brother!

When I ponder the times, the harvest of financial spending on two wars and (whoever got paid for them), I consider this new request for '700 Billion' more? Foreclosures, a brand new kind of 'homelessness'; unemployment; recession; depression; stock market crash; but,— in all that I see, I hear no voice speaking of the 'foot' that the Internal Revenue Services has placed upon the average taxpayer whose lives have changed so tremendously while bearing the burden of these payments. During my audit 'I wept', as Jesus did knowing that I would die trying to meet the burden that the IRS has placed upon my life— I die so that ??? might live in billion dollar houses! As I have heard so many others tell the same story, I 'rebuke this sin'— HEY SOMEBODY, ANYBODY, I NEED TO BE BAILED OUT, TOO!

What a God-fearing task is given the Christian disciple here in being 'so on guard' against sin in our own (Christian) nation that we are able to 'epitimeson/rebuke' sin in Iraq and Afghanistan! It is no small thing that after hearing these things the disciples would petition Jesus— *'increase our faith'!* ■

An Invitation to Study Bible Thursdays. 6:30 pm mustardseedfaith@bellsouth.net

---

October 3, 2008

Faith of a mustard seed
by Barbara Woods-Washington, M. Div.

"If you had faith as a grain of mustard seed, you could say to this sycamine tree, 'Be rooted up, and be planted in the sea,' and it would obey you." (Luke 17:6)

Luke's seventh use of 'pistis/faith' is Jesus' immediate response to the apostles' petition— *"Increase our faith!"* A double tradition, recorded also by Matthew (17:20), the variations include: a present tense subjunctive— for Matt *"if you have faith"*, while for Luke this subjunctive is past tense, *"if you had faith"* (simple, but key for me). This faith in Matt is 're-moving power' faith to speak to a mountain; while in Luke it is 'trans-planting power' faith to speak to a sycamine tree.

Redaction Criticism is a discipline in the field of Bible that is concerned with the theology of the writer of a given book. Both Old and New Testament Redaction scholars look at the author's 'point of view' revealed in the collection, arrangement, editing and modification of his sources. Not so easily dismissed when we consider having already looked at the fact that each and every one of us has a theology (whether examined, articulated or not) and that our 'sources' is one of the four components that 'give life' to 'my word', 'my view' of G(g)od—(G)old, (O)il, (D)rugs)??? in whom we say "We Trust!"

Barbara Woods Riles Washington

Luke, then, has given New Testament Redaction scholars a run for their money. So very articulate in his faith statement that he writes his two book work to 'theophilos'— commanding the attention of both the theologian and philosopher alike. His collection, arrangement, editing and modification of his sources sets him so far apart from Matthew

"The Voice Of A Proud Community"
Nashville P*R*I*D*E
Pulpit, Pew and Public

and Mark that while he is the most easily known as a writing personality, he causes the most problems for the traditional Bible scholar. The 17th Chapter of Luke has 3 uses of 'pistis/faith', 2 of which are single traditions— recorded only by Luke.

"If you had faith..." — a subjunctive in the past tense that for me is a reminder to continue to look back over life. The saying is sure that 'you can't know where you are going until you know where you have been'. It is not a 'crying over spilt milk', but a looking at the downfalls, the failures, and seeing the lost possibilities of the outcome had it been 'done in faith'. Not simply a 'where would I be' but an informing of each new action of 'where could I be'!

Nothing about the text of this double tradition is the same— for Matt it is a part of the 'Fig Tree' teaching while for Luke it follows the 'On Forgiveness' teaching... not just of our brother... but, of our self! It is 'trans-planting power' faith; although the action has 'been planted, and rooted, it can still be 'trans-planted' and 're-rooted'... even to the most remote and unknown parts... the sea! *"If you had faith!"* ■

An Invitation to Study Bible
Thursdays, 6:30 pm
mustardseedfaith@bellsouth.net

October 10, 2008

Faith of a mustard seed
by Barbara Woods-Washington, M. Div.

"Then one of them, when he saw that he was healed, turned back, praising God with a loud voice; and he fell on his face at Jesus' feet, giving him thanks. Now he was a Samaritan. Then said Jesus, "Were not ten cleansed? Where are the nine? Was no one found to return and give praise to God except this foreigner?" And he said to him, "rise and go your way; your faith has made you well." (Luke 17:15-19) Luke's eighth use of 'pistis/faith' is the single tradition recording of **'The Healing of Ten Lepers'**. Luke, again, stands alone in the telling of this miracle healing faith event in the life and ministry of Jesus. Noteworthy is the returning leper *"falling on his face"*.

One of my favorite Bibles for study is The *'Oxford Complete Parallel Bible with the Apocryphal/ Deuterocanonical Books'*. It is so very handy in that it is an interlinear of four well used English Translations: NRSV=New Revised Standard Version; REB=Revised English Bible; NAB=New American Bible; and the NJB=New Jerusalem Bible. There is no exchange for having the Apocryphal, especially the Books of The Maccabees available for reading. Yet, this tool is complete, for me, only with the additional use of The *'Interpreter's Bible'* which interlinears the KJV=King James Version and the RSV=(original)Revised Standard Version.

In case you missed this, we are talking six (6) English Translations of scripture! Of which, yours may or may not be included. I believe that every Christian should 'know all/ or something?' about the translators of 'your Bible'. That

Barbara Woods Riles Washington

"The Voice Of A Proud Community"
Nashville P*R*I*D*E
Pulpit, Pew and Public

said, a closer look is needed in seeing the faith of the returning leper 'falling on his face'.

The discussion on the meaning of 'prosopon/face' as used here is one that we take for granted in our modern religiosity. To be sure, the 'seeking God's face' gave meaning to daily living in the Old Testament. The 'face', the 'countenance', the 'presence' of God, the 'face to face' encounter with God is the prayer and longing of the believer in securing the grace and peace given in a right relationship with God.

When I first entered the Seminary I was in my days of 'cover girl'— so professional in my daily make-up ritual. One day I was accosted in the hall by a young man of the ??? persuasion who put his finger in my face 'to rebuke the sin', as he saw it, in the 'lipstick' (et al) on my face. Needless to say he 'got out of my face'! But within the following year of Biblical studies, I came to learn the importance of the face as it relates to 'countenance'. I have not used make-up on my face since then.

When we consider all the studies done on the face— 'Chinese Face Wisdom' teachings; 'Eyes of Wisdom' teachings, nose, mouth, teeth, et al, there is something greater to be said about this act of 'contrition' this act of respect, humility, homage and veneration— 'falling on one's face'. To surrender the most important part of the body— while in praise and thanksgiving to God for cleansing from disease.

Ten were healed. One came back. But then, 'face to face'... with Jesus, he 'falls on his face'!■

An Invitation to Study Bible Thursdays. 6:30 pm mustardseedfaith@bellsouth.net

---

October 17, 2008

Faith of a mustard seed
by Barbara Woods-Washington, M. Div.

"Then said Jesus, "Were not ten cleansed? Where are the nine? Was no one found to return and give praise to God except this foreigner?" And he said to him, "rise and go your way; your faith has made you well." (Luke 17:17-19).

Hard to leave Luke's eighth use of 'pistis/faith', this single tradition recording of **'The Healing of Ten Lepers'** without taking a look at the 'praise' theme. This 'one of ten', the 'talented tenth' the 'grateful tenth' turned back when he saw that he had been healed, and he praised God with a loud voice.

'Doxa/glory' stands in this text's translation of 'praise'. The oldest and most concrete meaning of 'doxa' has the sense of 'light' or 'radiance'. Where in the Old Testament it very early has the sense of something 'weighty' in (hu)man(ity) which gives him importance, honor— (referenced by his riches, wealth, prestige); it soon develops from glory or honor ascribed to man to a complete transference to God. The term 'doxa', in an unexplained shift in it's meaning, is now only found in an expression of the 'divine nature', 'power' and 'honour' given only to God. Glory is given by God to man, but man must give his glory back to God!

Barbara Woods Riles Washington

To be sure, it is the Psalmist who so poetically gives meaning to this term as it rings throughout the book—*"But Thou, O Lord, art a shield for me, my glory, and the lifter up of mine head."*; *"The heavens declare the glory of God, ..."*; *"His glory is great in thy salvation: honor and majesty hast thou laid upon him."*; *"Ascribe to the Lord the glory due his name..."*; *"The Lord is high above all nations and his glory above the heavens."*;

"The Voice Of A Proud Community"
Nashville P*R*I*D*E
Pulpit, Pew and Public

"Not to us, O Lord, not to us, but to thy name give glory, for the sake of thy steadfast love and thy faithfulness!"

By New Testament times, 'doxa/glory' is strictly used to express 'the divine mode' of being. Jesus references Soloman *'in all of his glory...'*, but yet, when The 'doxa/glory' of The Lord is shone 'round about' the Shepherds who kept watch over their flock by night, it made them afraid.

Sometimes I feel like a foreigner in a Church where Christians can't quite get the meaning of 'doxa/ glory/ praise'. Is the Church so bound by it's tradition that it is unable to see the Glory of the Lord shining 'round about' it? Church, like the Shepherds— 'so afraid'. Call me 'holier than thou???' Call me crazy, but, let me tell you, praise(ing God with a loud voice)... is what I do!

Ten Churches— and 'His Glory' can only be seen and felt in one! Ten Homes— only one! Ten Christians? Ten Lives? Ten Lepers! Were not Ten cleansed? Where are the Nine?■

An Invitation to Study Bible
Thursdays. 6:30 pm
mustardseedfaith@bellsouth.net

October 24, 2008

Faith of a mustard seed
by Barbara Woods-Washington, M. Div.

"And he told them a parable to the effect that they ought always to pray and not loose heart. He said, "In a certain city there was a judge who neither feared God nor regarded man; and there was a widow in that city who kept coming to him and saying 'Vindicate me against my adversary.' For a while he refused; but afterwards he said to himself, 'Though I neither fear God nor regard man, yet because this widow bothers me, I will vindicate her, or she will wear me out by her continual coming.'" And the Lord said, "Hear what the unrighteous judge says. And will not God vindicate his elect, who cry to him day and night? Will he delay long over them? I tell you, he will vindicate them speedily. Nevertheless, when the Son of man comes, will he find faith on earth?" (Luke 18:1-8).*

Barbara Woods Riles Washington

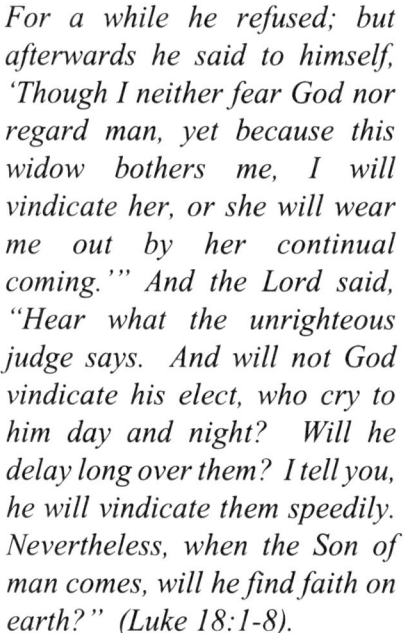

Luke's ninth use of 'pistis/faith' is a single tradition parable, known as **'The Unjust Judge'**. With no parallel, it is one of several Lucan parables that give a glimpse into the Gospel writers theology. As a prologue to this parable, Luke has indicated that it's effect should be in direct relationship to 'proseuchomai/prayer' (without ceasing) and 'egkakeo/not loose heart'; the combination of which raises a question for Jesus in the pronouncement portion of this parable— when I come, will I find it on earth?

To distinguish 'proseuchomai/prayer' from the various other words used for prayer in New Testament scripture, this word is more indicative of prayer as 'phenomenon'; 'a lifestyle'; to 'call on God' without content or intent; 'a piousness'. To live in a 'state of prayerfulness'— *"My House shall be called a House of Prayer"!* It is not a 'petition' or 'asking' when in need. It is not a small thing that when trouble comes, when sickness and adversity comes, the believer and the non-believer alike 'call on the same God' and in many instances it becomes the conversion point in the life of the non-believer. 'Proseuchomai/prayer' , then, has the sense of calling on God for presence at all times, allowing the Will of God to be done without having to indicate to an omniscient God what needs to be done. It's 'lifestyle'— it's 'homestyle'!

What we see simply as 'loose heart', is of far greater consequence than what meets the eye. The word in this text, 'egkakeo/not loose heart' has at it's root 'kakos/evil'! In raising the 'problem of evil' in this parable, Luke has opened the door to a major discussion for our times. Contrary to the ever popular belief and teaching (in the Christian Church???) on an 'external source' of (d)evil/Satan???— Jesus has clearly regarded the (hu)man heart as the source and seat of evil! When the Heads (of Nation, of State, of Church, of Household, of School) does evil, the effect is that— 'when I would do good, I too...'!

House your life in a state of prayerfulness and DO NOT 'egkakeo'— 'loose heart'; 'do evil'; 'mistreat'; 'act badly'; 'grow weary'! A brand new and pointed, yet old and simple definition of faith! Yet, Jesus questions whether he will find this, not just in the Church, the Nation— but, 'where in the world?. ■

*An Invitation to Study Bible
Thursdays, 6:30 pm
mustardseedfaith@bellsouth.net*

October 31, 2008

Faith of a mustard seed
by Barbara Woods-Washington, M. Div.

"For a while he refused; but afterwards he said to himself, 'Though I neither fear God nor regard man, yet because this widow bothers me, I will vindicate her, or she will wear me out by her continual coming'." And the Lord said, "Hear what the unrighteous judge says. And will not God vindicate his elect, who cry to him day and night? Will he delay long over them? I tell you, he will vindicate them speedily. Nevertheless, when the Son of man comes, will he find faith on earth?" (Luke 18:4-8). A second look at Luke's ninth use of 'pistis/faith', this single tradition parable—**'The Unjust Judge'**.

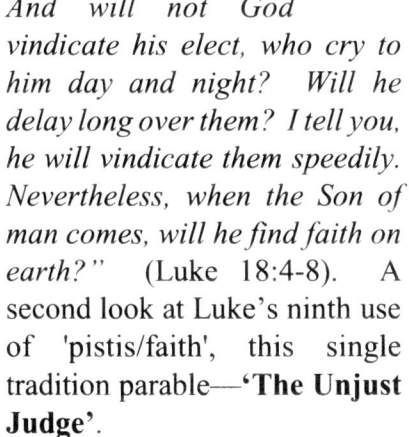

The 'Fear of God' is a major theme of Old Testament faith and is a teaching found throughout the Biblical Wisdom Books. To be sure, as it is written— 'The Fear of God IS the beginning of Wisdom'. In the ancient Greek pantheon, 'Phobos' /Fear IS a god who is both real and powerful. The deity Phobos is the one who 'causes terror' and is placed just after Zeus and before all other gods.

Barbara Woods Riles Washington

By New Testament, the concept 'phobos/fear' has had a long history and always denotes 'a reaction' when (hu)man encounters force. This reaction is tied to emotions which run a range of senses from— 'terror'; 'anxiety'; 'flight'; startle'; to— 'respect'; 'awe'; 'honour'; and even 'reverence'. The 'Fear of God' as it brings wisdom and knowledge into a life, bestows an inheritance of protection, direction, guidance, counsel and peace which enables that life to fear nothing other than God. This Judge, by his own admission, had no terror, no fear, no awe, no honour, no reverence for God.

"The Voice Of A Proud Community"
Nashville P*R*I*D*E
Pulpit, Pew and Public

Not only does this official say of himself that he neither fears god and, also— he has no regard for man! Having been elected or selected to this position to serve men, he is moved to respond to the needs of his people only when they reach the point of nuisance in persistence, 'continual coming'. At this point it becomes about him— *'she will wear me out!'*

I am so tempted to speak of our times and 'elected officials' whose every act is 'all about self'! Armed robbery with no fear of God and no regard for men which, for the every day man, would bring judgement, indictment and imprisonment.

We look at one official and call for impeachment holding a trial for 'crimes of passion'; wherein the injury is only done to the individual by way of pride and character. Then we turn our heads on another official who has yet to be tried for 'crimes of war' and 'armed robbery' of his entire nation's financial resources wherein the injury is done to millions in the loss of life; home; on and on and on. But, you do the math.

It is no small thing that in a rare occurrence, Jesus uses an adjective to speak of a biblical character— in this case, this Judge, Luke records Jesus saying, is 'adikias/unrighteous'.

Aristotle's Ethics describes the 'adikias' as 'a violator of law'; which is soon used for those who 'uphold the law as violators of law'. Once the concept enters the religious sphere most particularly the Judeo-Christian tradition where 'The Law' is of major concern, the 'adikias', the unrighteous, the unjust, is the 'violator of divine law'. And the Lord said, *"Hear what the unrighteous judge says."*

His offense is no longer just against man, but now against God. Oh, but that's right. This Judge has already admitted that he has no regard for God or man! ■

An Invitation to Study Bible
Thursdays. 6:30 pm
mustardseedfaith@bellsouth.net

November 7, 2008

Faith of a mustard seed
by Barbara Woods-Washington, M. Div.

"And the Lord said, "Hear what the unrighteous judge says. And will not God vindicate his elect, who cry to him day and night? Will he delay long over them? I tell you, he will vindicate them speedily. Nevertheless, when the Son of man comes, will he find faith on earth?" (Luke 18:6-8). A final look at Luke's ninth use of 'pistis/faith', this single tradition parable—**'The Unjust Judge'**.

How to look at 'The Parable' as a phenomenal form of teaching has posed a problem for Biblical Scholars historically. Jeremias in his major work on <u>'The Parables Of Jesus'</u> is definitive in stating that the parables are "weapons of controversy"; and identified no usage of 'the parable' (as defined by the field of Biblical Form Criticism) in the Rabbinic tradition prior to Jesus. To be sure, so often called 'Rabbi', it is clear that the persons of his times regarded highly the teaching ministry of Jesus.

Seeing and hearing— but without understanding, is a constant reminder on the part of Jesus as he goes about the task of teaching his message of 'God's Kingdom Come'! For those who do see, who do hear, who do understand— the parabolic message is 'keys to The Kingdom'. For all others it remains in parable.

Some scholars have been deliberate in showing another critical aspect of the character and nature of 'the parable'. Dodd saw a 'bottom line' theme recurring in a large core of The Parables and determined the need to see the 'bottom line' despite the temptation to be lost in the elements of allegory. It is to this bottom line that Jeremias speaks in saying that "every one of them calls for an answer on the spot."

Barbara Woods Riles Washington

"The Voice Of A Proud Community"
Nashville P*R*I*D*E
Pulpit, Pew and Public

✝ 87

This parable, 'The Unjust Judge' or 'The Unrighteous Judge' is one where there can be little doubt of the importance of the bottom line. Luke has recorded Jesus as dismissing the 'set-up' portion, to bring the eye and the ear to the 'bottom line'— "Nevertheless (about the other stuff), see this, hear this, *"when the Son of man comes, will he find faith on earth?"*

One of my most important memories of my grandmother, 'the faith keeper' of our family, was a Sunday morning close of Worship as we greeted the Pastor at the door. She reviewed to him something that he had said in his message and invited him to come to Sunday School to repeat it. I learned from her to be completely attentive to the preaching ministry— (we got that 'notorious pinch' which took 'a plug' out of you if you so much as stirred while the preacher was preaching). I do so even today. I learned also that the relevance of the teaching ministry when applied could, and I think should, cause controversy. But, persons of controversy who are there, like Jesus, to 'stir up the gifts', are no longer welcomed in the Church; but, neither do persons of controversy, like Jesus, 'feel at home' in this (Church)— any more.

While it is next to void when it comes to New Testament commentaries on this parable of 'The Unjust Judge', I commend to you an application of it's direct relationship to our national life in your teaching ministry. But not without the 'bottom line'— would the Son of Man be able to see your faith?■

*An Invitation to Study Bible
Thursdays, 6:30 pm
mustardseedfaith@bellsouth.net*

November 14, 2008

Faith of a mustard seed
by Barbara Woods-Washington, M. Div.

"As he drew near to Jericho, a blind man was sitting by the roadside begging; and hearing a multitude going by, he inquired what this meant. They told him, "Jesus of Nazareth is passing by." And he cried, "Jesus, Son of David, have mercy on me!" And those who were in front rebuked him, telling him to be silent; but he cried out all the more, "Son of David, have mercy on me!" And Jesus stopped, and commanded him to be brought to him; and when he came near, he asked him, "What do you want me to do for you?" He said, "Lord, let me receive my sight." And Jesus said to him, "Receive your sight; your faith has made you well." (Luke 18:35-42).

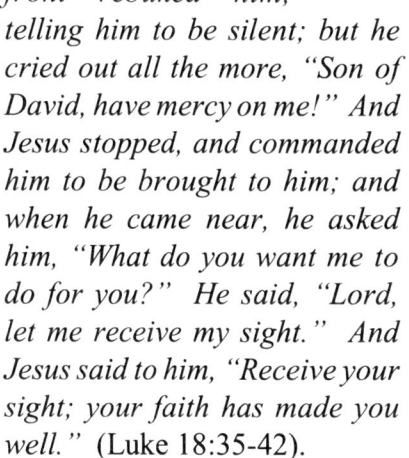

Luke's tenth use of 'pistis/faith' is a triple tradition pericope known as **'The Healing Of The Blind Man At Jericho'**. Variations reveal first that it is not a faith occurrence for Matthew. Unnamed, two blind men cry out to Jesus asking for their 'eyes to be opened'. And for Matthew, this restoration of sight for these two men was an 'act of pity'. Mark has named a single man as a 'blind beggar, Bartimaeus' who 'has heard' that Jesus is the reason for the multitude gathering. For Luke this blind beggar is unnamed and 'he hears' the multitude— and inquires as to the reason for it's gathering.

Needless to say that the best of the best of New Testament theologians see major problems with this Lucan text; with again— void commentary! To be sure some, including Bultmann, suggests it to be a 'creation of the early Christian Community' to further the question of it's historic authenticity. The discussion

Barbara Woods Riles Washington

✝ 88

"The Voice Of A Proud Community"
Nashville P*R*I*D*E
Pulpit, Pew and Public

centers around the use of the title for Jesus by the blind man— 'Jesus, Son of David', which has it's first occurrence here for Luke.

I received the news story this week by email of WAPT news' coverage of two Pearl (Mississippi) Jr. High School students being put off their school bus for saying: "Barack Obama is our President!" With 'video proof' from the bus, school officials released the statement that the employees 'over reacted' and appropriate action is being taken.

Something in this title 'Jesus, Son of David' caused an 'over reaction'! Time and space does not permit here a righteous examination of the 'Messianic Hope' contained in the title used by this blind beggar— *"Jesus, Son of David"*. Only that a man with 'no sight', with keen sense of 'hearing' knew that something was going on and when he came to know 'who' was in this crowd' he cried out to him with a title that released rebuke. Having previously looked at 'rebuke/epitimao' we see that the form used here is most always used by (hu)man. Then, at best, with limited capabilities. In man's use of rebuke there is the sense of threat, blame, punishment and even superiority— but not without a response from Jesus.

"... but he cried out all the more, "Son of David, have mercy on me!" I did say that man's rebuke has 'limited capabilities'— make you wanna hollar, throw up both your hands! After being rebuked, *"he cried out all the more, "Son of David, have mercy on me!"*

Jesus stopped, turned to him and said, *'What do you want me to do for you?"* ■

An Invitation to Study Bible Thursdays, 6:30 pm mustardseedfaith@bellsouth.net

---

November 21, 2008

Faith of a mustard seed
by Barbara Woods-Washington, M. Div.

"Jesus stopped and ordered the man to be brought to him. When he had drawn near, Jesus asked him, "What do you want me to do for you?" "Sir," he answered, "I want to see again." Jesus said to him, "Regain your sight! Your faith has brought you salvation!" (Luke 18:40-42 The Anchor Bible). A second look at Luke's tenth use of 'pistis/faith': **'The Healing Of The Blind Man At Jericho'**.

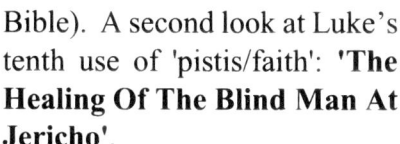

Michaelis has studied the numerous words used in the Greek language for the verb 'to see'. He reminds us that there are so many verbs for our simple English translation 'to see'; used to cover such a wide range of meaning that it clearly indicates the high estimation that seeing has in the life of (hu)man. To be sure, Greek religions are regarded by many as 'religions of vision'. It is no small thing that Jesus, in ministry to a Greek speaking world, would also throughout his teachings emphasize— yea specialize in the need 'to see'.

Barbara Woods Riles Washington

'Blepo' the term used here for 'to see' is used three times in this text with each occurrence being the form 'anablepo/to see again'. The blind man, being brought to Jesus, notwithstanding the 'hold-up' attempt by the crowd, received 'one wish' which was— *"I want to see again!"* Jesus grants this wish in the imperative mood of command— *"See Again!"* And at once, Luke records, *"He saw again!"*

'Blepo', then, has a stronger emphasis on the function of the eye in relation to the sense of seeing. It is a return from 'short-sightedness'; it is 'to have insight'; it is 'conceptual perception'. In Matthew's 13th Chapter's 'Parable of the Sower', Jesus says to the disciples, *"the*

"The Voice Of A Proud Community"
Nashville P*R*I*D*E
Pulpit, Pew and Public

reason I speak to them in Parables is that 'blepontes/seeing' they do not percieve..." Look—Again, at this healing of the blind man and see that it is not the physical sight that is being wished for, it is clearly something that he once had, but has now lost— *"Lord I want to see Again."*

I am reminded of how easy it is to loose sight of 'whatsoever is just'; 'whatsoever is pure.. whatsoever is true...' surrounded by systems that eat alive those who enter walking in justice, in purity and truth. During my years as a student at Tennessee State University, I 'marched' several times to the Capital as the community protested 'take-overs'. Now it is a community 'taken over' with little or no knowledge or protest as to what takes place in the Capital. *"Lord I NEED TO SEE— AGAIN."*

It is the same verb used by Jesus when *'The Sinful Woman'* came to Simon's house to anoint Jesus with her alabaster of ointment. Jesus said "Simeon 'blepeis/you see' this woman?" It is not the verb used for visionary, not for glance, not for physical sightedness, nor for prophesy— just a clear and simple sense of the faces, the spaces; the realities of the interconnectedness of life— right around you.

This 'wish', this 'petition' made by the blind man in this text has become a daily prayer for my life: *"Lord,"* (I wish I had a praying Church...) *"I want to see again."* To 'see clearly' is a perception that enables one to know 'a lie' the minute CNN or FoxNews reports it! I like the way John put it, read his lips— *"and you will know the truth... and the truth will set you free!"* ■

An Invitation to Study Bible Thursdays, 6:30 pm mustardseedfaith@bellsouth.net

November 28, 2008

Faith of a mustard seed
by Barbara Woods-Washington, M. Div.

'**Peter's Denial Prophesied**' is a triple tradition pericope set by all three Gospel writers at the Mount of Olives. Peculiar to Luke are two verses embedded in his account of this event; and is for him alone an occurrence of 'pistis/faith'— his eleventh and final use in his Gospel. *"Simon, Simon, behold Satan demanded to have you, that he might sift you like wheat, but I have prayed for you that your faith may not fail; and when you have turned again, strengthen your brethren."* (Luke 22:31-32).

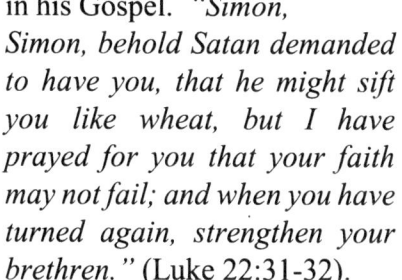

As a New Testament Student during my first year in Seminary, I was challenged on every hand by the work of Rudolf Bultmann. First with his awesome work entitled '**Primitive Christianity**' which was required reading for the course New Testament History; then with discovering his work entitled '**Kerygma and Myth**' (where Kerygma is 'the preaching of the early Church'). It is here that I begin this discussion on 'satanology'. At the risk of over simplifying, he makes these statements: "The cosmology of the New Testament is essentially mythical in character. The world is viewed as a three storied structure. ...Man is not in control of his own life. Evil spirits may take possession of him. Satan may inspire him with evil thoughts." After a complete sobering statement of Christian Mythology, (Christology), he says "Can Christian preaching expect modern man to accept the mythical view of the world as true? To do so would be both senseless and impossible. ...no man can adopt a view of the world by his own volition— it is already determined for him by his place in history."

Barbara Woods Riles Washington

"The Voice Of A Proud Community"
Nashville P*R*I*D*E
Pulpit, Pew and Public

I am most informed in my thinking on the place that 'satan' has in my theology by the Old Testament course Job which I studied under the late Dr. G. Murray Branch who, during my years with him he also served as Pastor to the historic Sixteenth Street Baptist Church in Birmingham. So convinced am I of the importance of the Book of **Job** in Christology that in most all Churches that I have taught Bible Study across the years, I have begun the study with the Book of Job. Significant to point out here that Old Testament scholarship has long separated the Prologue/Epilogue from the body of the book which can clearly be seen based upon cosmological view alone. Having done so, you will not find a single reference to 'satan' in the original body text of The Book of Job. Biblical studies have identified the origins of the 'Prologue/Epilogue of Job' as 'post-exilic'— originating during the Babylonian exile while under the thought and influence of Babylonian Religions. A place where the question is raised: "how can we sing the Lord's song in a strange land!" Bultmann is on target with his "task of demythologogizing the new testament proclamation"!

A difficult task indeed. I attended a Wednesday night Bible Study session at Spruce Street Church here in Nashville where the discussion leader's entire discourse was on the 'power of satan' with heads bobbing in affirmation. After some time, I interjected with this statement, "in the oldest biblical faith traditions of Old Testament, there is no satan! God is the author of both good and evil." The 'beat down' came swift and sure. With no personal investment, I continue to move on. ∎

An Invitation to Study Bible Thursdays. 6:30 pm mustardseedfaith@bellsouth.net

December 5, 2008

Faith of a mustard seed
by Barbara Woods-Washington, M. Div.

Most urgent of the tasks given at Christmas, I believe, is the charge given to the Wise Men by King Herrod. *"Then he sent them to Bethlehem saying, "Go and search diligently for the child; and when you have found him, bring me word so that I may also go and pay him homage."* (Matthew 2:8)

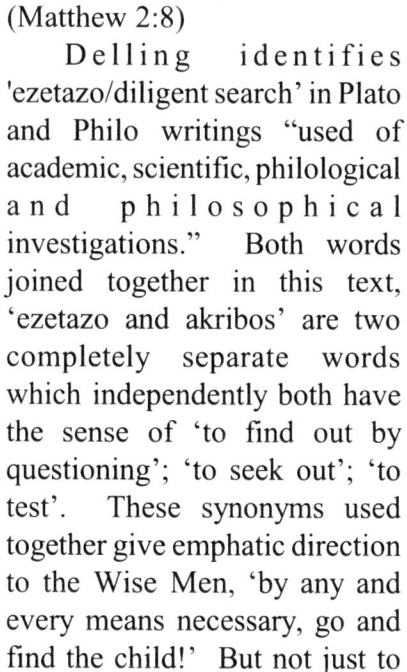

Delling identifies 'ezetazo/diligent search' in Plato and Philo writings "used of academic, scientific, philological and philosophical investigations." Both words joined together in this text, 'ezetazo and akribos' are two completely separate words which independently both have the sense of 'to find out by questioning'; 'to seek out'; 'to test'. These synonyms used together give emphatic direction to the Wise Men, 'by any and every means necessary, go and find the child!' But not just to 'find the child', but seek to know all there is to know about the child.

I am reminded of the exercise that the late great Reverend Dr. Howard Thurman gave us as we began our "seven day intensive study of the grounds and meaning of the religious experience." He gathered ten black seminarians from throughout the country (one of the two reasons given in our scholarship letter is that "we are black") and sat us around him as he was seated in a long leather lounge chaise. He had us to close our eyes as he walked us into a deep still silent place inside ourselves. Once there he said to write the first thing that comes to our mind when he said the next word. "JESUS". After listening to our individual associations he sat up from his chair and said to us, "Young people, don't spend your lives

Barbara Woods Riles Washington

"The Voice Of A Proud Community"
Nashville P*R*I*D*E
Pulpit, Pew and Public

† 93

putting so much on Jesus. Jesus is his own man. It just may be that God is calling you to be a Christ."

Critical to the task that Herrod has given the Wise Men is the 'warning' given to them in a dream— to go back another way. Change— the word of the century used as the theme to drive the most phenomenal election in American history. Change! We need!

I am convinced and have diligently sought to convince the church of the need to change the way we handle 'the child' that is given. My statement continues now as a part of every sermon that I prepare and deliver: "TIME OUT for volunteer workers with the children in the church. TIME IN for full time Children's Pastors and full time Children's Ministries to meet the ever growing needs and demands of the lives of children in our times. One thing that puzzles me greatly is how easily we have succumbed to the plot to put 5 year olds on 'drugs' as they enter the school systems???? What kind of rehabilitation can be given in this life as it grows into adulthood? Better question— is there life after (this forced drug addiction) death (of an innocent child)?

One of my program visions for Children's Ministries is one that is beyond 'nursery school' and 'day care'— but a church program for 4 year olds at risk for the system's 'Ritalin'; or 'Adderall' et al, drug addictions. Needless to say, it is not in 'The Church Budget!!!' (Where your treasure Is...).

The 'Warning' is one that must be heeded— when it comes to 'the Way' that we have taken to seek 'the child', *"Go back another way!"* ■

An Invitation to Study Bible Thursdays. 6:30 pm mustardseedfaith@bellsouth.net

---

December 26, 2008

Faith of a mustard seed
by Barbara Woods-Washington, M. Div.

"Simon, Simon, behold Satan demanded to have you, that he might sift you like wheat, but I have prayed for you that your faith may not fail; and when you have turned again, strengthen your brethren." (Luke 22:31-32).

While in Seminary, I was unaware of the fact that so many of my professors served also as pastors. I knew that my Old Testament Professor, Dr. John Waters was Pastor to the Solid Rock Baptist Church and that my Mission of The Church professor, Dr. George Thomas was Pastor to the Shaw Temple (Faith) AME Zion Church (both in Atlanta) because each had invited me to preach on special days at these two Churches. But of those who had pastorates out of town, I had no first hand knowledge. I discovered my Old Testament professor, Dr. G. Murray Branch's pastorate while reading a magazine and seeing a full page ad of him standing on the steps of the Dexter Avenue (King Memorial) Baptist Church in Montgomery (not the Sixteenth Street Church in Birmingham as previously stated).

Barbara Woods Riles Washington

Looking again at Luke's eleventh and final use of 'pistis/faith' in his Gospel; the discussion on 'satanology' as informed by Dr. Branch's course on the Book Of Job.

To understand God as the author of both good and evil is to stand deep and strong in the heart of the Old Testament faith tradition. I like the analogy of the pyramid as an image for seeing that there are two points to every side which progressively come closer together until the top reveals a single, solitary point! This point, alone, is a God that is omnipotent (having all power); who is omniscient (knowing all

☦ 95

The Voice Of A Proud Community
Nashville P*R*I*D*E
Pulpit, Pew and Public

things); and who is omnipresent (actively present in all times and in all places). I am convinced that it is by 'choice' that one comes to see God at this highest level of life! Revelation, yes (chicken or the egg?). But, when you choose to sit on *'The Mourners Pew'* and choose to stay there long enough— revelation will come. Som'in 'bout 'that pew' that leaves it empty in most every Church that I go into for services in our times. There is no longer the teaching nor the practice. The vitality of this 'born againness' pew, this deliverance pew, this revelatory faith tradition his been lost on the Church.

You can chose god at any point of the pyramid image, but any point below THE single and solitary TOP, will require you to work out and rationalize your opposite point— your (god's) 'enemy', your 'satan'. (Kinda' schizophrenic by nature? Do you want to be made whole?). In my Philosophy of Religion course I used an interview done on Rabbi Adin Steinsaltz entitled **'The Vertical Adventure'** where the Rabbi speaks of our inheriting a 'skyscraper' and our choosing to live on the ground floor and basement rather than make our way to life at the top. Som'in about this spiritual— "I'm gonna lay down my (burdens) my sword and shield, down by the Riverside...! I ain't gon study war no more!. I ain't gon study war no more!. I ain't gon study war no more!". Our newly elected President has inherited a 'complete curriculum' of war and his (and our) expectations of "Change" condescends to the demands now placed upon his life— 'to study war!'

As for me, it's a conscious decision— at THE TOP is ONLY GOD! I ain't gon study satanology no more!. In this small, atomic, neutronic space in time in which I live it will forever be "God (that) made me do it!" ■

An Invitation to Study Bible Thursdays, 6:30 pm
mustardseedfaith@bellsouth.net

January 9, 2009

Faith of a mustard seed
by Barbara Woods-Washington, M. Div.

"... but I have prayed for you that your faith may not fail; and when you have turned again, strengthen your brethren." (Luke 22:32). Another look at Luke's Single tradition verse embedded in the Triple tradition **'Peter's Denial Prophesied'**— his eleventh and final occurrence of 'pistis/faith'.

I hope that you, like I, am beginning to recognize the significance of this directed study of the occurrences of the word 'pistis' as English translations of scripture use 'faith'. Thus far it has been used most specifically in the Gospel's sayings, teaching and ministry of Jesus. Several rare concepts have been identified in conjunction with it's usage. And here, again, a very rare concept is used.

Jesus says to Peter, I have 'edeithen/prayed' for you that your 'pistis/faith' may not 'eklipe/fail'— where both word forms used for 'prayed' and for 'fail' are so rare that Young's has not identified either.

Needless to say again that the problems with this text persists in that it is a verse that is only recorded by Luke, a saying which appears as a 'pop-up' in 'Peter's Denial Prophesied' recorded also by Matthew and Mark. Subsequently, 'this prayer' is one that is difficult to get a handle on. What is it about this prayer that Jesus prayed that makes it 'stand alone' in scripture with no parallel?

Kittle places 'edeithen/prayed' among the 'deisis' word study group; first used for 'specific prayer in concrete situations'. 'Eklipe/fail' is placed among the 'dokimos' word study group which has the sense of 'tested in battle'; 'reliable'; 'trustworthy'; 'certifiable'; 'to find worthy';

Barbara Woods Riles Washington

"The Voice Of A Proud Community"
Nashville P*R*I*D*E
Pulpit, Pew and Public

☦ 96

'proven valuable'. While instances are found in secular Greek, Grundmann suggests that it first acquires religious significance in the New Testament and that in Pauline thought and usage of this concept "we are brought face to face with ideas that are peculiar to the New Testament".

The small stuff? A single prayer from Jesus found only one time in the entire realm of scripture: specific and concrete! Listen up Peter. You are about to be in the throes of great temptation. Your understanding of faith has not reached for THE single and solitary TOP where there is ONLY GOD! Your satan makes demands upon your life to which you will yield. You will be sifted as wheat. But, in this concrete situation, in this space in life time, I have prayed for you!! Not for your deliverance, you must go through—not for your salvation, not for your healing, not for your wealth, but, specifically, concretely that 'your faith may not fail'. I pray for you, Peter, that you will have a faith 'tested in battle'. A faith that is 'reliable'; 'trustworthy'; and 'certifiable'. A faith 'to find worthy'; and 'proven valuable'. ■

An Invitation to Study Bible
Thursdays. 6:30 pm
mustardseedfaith@bellsouth.net

January 16, 2009

Faith of a mustard seed
by Barbara Woods-Washington, M. Div.

What has Luke said concerning 'faith/pistis'? Eleven clear references given to the understanding of faith.

1st the Triple tradition **'Healing of the Paralytic'**. Introducing 'faith/pistis' as 'controversy'! *"When he saw their faith, he said, "Man, your sins are forgiven you." "Who is this who is speaking blasphemies?"* The strongest form of personal mockery and calumniation; it always refers finally to god. *"He who blasphemes the name of the Lord shall be put to death." "We have seen strange things today".*

2nd is a return to **'The Centurion's Servant'**. Something in 'the cotton' in this very rare translation of 'o pais mou'; for a look at the Greek text would definitively suggest the titles "The Centurion's Son" or "The Centurion's Boy". CENTURION'S SLAVE SON (or daughter)! The centurion's servant boy (or girl)! So great was this man's will for the healing of this boy that Jesus said, *"Not even in Israel have I seen such faith!"*

3rd **'A Sinful Woman Forgiven'**. Necessary to examine separate and apart from 'amartia/sin'; 'amartolos/sinner' as an adjective. Sin as 'a power hostile to God'— sinner now becomes a value judgement from the human standpoint. Rare in Classical Greek. Clear picture of 'the sinner' from the Psalmist. He is the opposite of the 'pious, righteous and godly'. He breaks the commandments and trust in his own power and wealth and understanding. Simon had a 'difference made bigger' in his mind— he a Pharisee and she a sinner. He talked to himself saying, 'if Jesus were a prophet He would already know!' No

Barbara Woods Riles Washington

☥ 97

"The Voice Of A Proud Community"
Nashville P*R*I*D*E
Pulpit, Pew and Public

apparent sickness or disease in her life— yet, Jesus gives the same pronouncement *"your sins are forgiven"*!

4th the triple tradition **'Calming Of The Storm'** (Luke 8:22-25). The disciples fear was so great in the midst of this storm of the sea, this 'ekindunenon/ danger', that they repeated their call out to the Lord— *"Master, Master..."* And the response is still the same... *"Where Is Your Faith?"*

5th the triple tradition **'A Woman's Faith'.** Even with her matchless faith which gave her 'heart' to go up and touch Jesus to receive her healing, this woman was 'covered' by the crowd which enabled her to 'think' that she was 'hidden' from Jesus. Ashamed at not speaking up when he asked, it was not until 'He saw her' that "she came forth trembling..."

6th **'On Causing Sin'** and **'On Forgiveness'**— Luke stands alone in recording the petition, *"Increase our faith!"* Jesus warns of a retribution 'worse than death' for the offender. You will (passively) 'skandalon/scandal', sin, stumble, fall, but— to be the cause (actively) of 'skandalon' carries with it a fate; for— *"It would be better for you if a millstone were hung around your neck and you were thrown into the sea".*

7th Jesus' immediate response to the apostles' petition— *"Increase our faith!"*; *"If you had faith as a grain of mustard seed, you could say to this sycamine tree, 'Be rooted up, and be planted in the sea,' and it would obey you."* It is 'trans-planting power' faith. Although the action has been planted, and rooted, it can still be 'trans-planted' and 're-rooted'... even to the most remote and unknown parts... the sea! *"If you had faith!"* ■

An Invitation to Study Bible
Thursdays. 6:30 pm
mustardseedfaith@bellsouth.net

January 23, 2009

Faith of a mustard seed
by Barbara Woods-Washington, M. Div.

8th the single tradition **'The Healing of Ten Lepers'**. The one returning leper *'falling on his face'*. The 'seeking God's face' gave meaning to daily living in the Old Testament. The 'face', the 'countenance', the 'presence' of God, the 'face to face' encounter with God is the prayer and longing of the believer in securing the grace and peace given in a right relationship with God. 'Falling on one's face'. To surrender the most important part of the body— while in praise and thanksgiving to God for cleansing from disease. Ten were healed. One came back. But then, 'face to face'... with Jesus, he *'falls on his face'*!

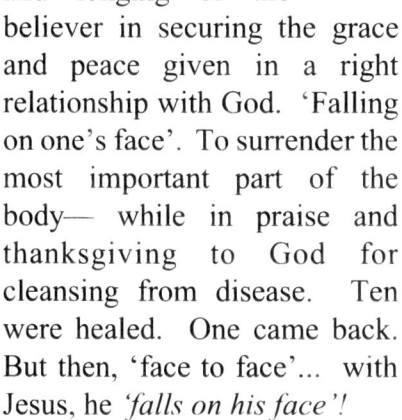

9th a single tradition parable,**'The Unjust Judge'**. Luke has indicated that it's effect should be in direct relationship to 'proseuchomai/prayer' (without ceasing) and 'egkakeo/not loose heart'. 'Egkakeo' has at it's root 'kakos/evil'! In raising the 'problem of evil' in this parable, this Judge, Luke records Jesus saying, is 'adikias/unrighteous' 'a violator of law'; which is soon used for those who 'uphold the law as violators of law'. *"When the Son of man comes, will he find faith on earth?"*

10th a triple tradition **'The Healing Of The Blind Man At Jericho'**. A man with 'no sight', with keen sense of 'hearing' knew that something was going on and when he came to know 'who' was in this crowd' he cried out to him with a title that released rebuke. Jesus stopped, turned to him and said, *'What do you want me to do for you?"* 'Blepo' the term used here for 'to see' is used three times in this text with each occurrence being the form 'anablepo/to see again'. Not the

Barbara Woods Riles Washington

The Voice Of A Proud Community
Nashville P*R*I*D*E
Pulpit, Pew and Public

physical sight that is being wished for, it is clearly something that he once had, but has now lost— *"Lord I want to see Again*!

11th is **'Peter's Denial Prophesied'**. You can chose god at any point of the pyramid image, but any point below THE single and solitary TOP, will require you to work out and rationalize your opposite point— your 'enemy', your 'satan'. (Kinda' schizophrenic by nature?) Do you want to be made whole?

In this the final use of 'pistis/faith', it is noteworthy to see in 'epistrephas' the word used here for 'turned again'— the root, 'pist/ in faith! Never could have seen it based upon translation. (True meaning of the saying 'lost in translation'). To be sure it is a compound word, 'epistrephas', which has a long history by the time we see Luke as the primary user in New Testament. It has the sense of 'to convert'; 'to change'; 'to turn one's attention to'; 'to pay regard to'. 'To return to the ground of being or to oneself'; 'necessary change in inner attitude'. And when you have... strengthen your Brethren. 'Sterison'— "to make fast'; 'to support'; 'to fix so that it stands upright and immovable'; 'make firm'; 'ground'; 'hold steadfast'. Over and over again I am confronted with persons whom I knew (or whom I thought I knew before their 'rise to power??")— forget to remember! Peter, I know that you will 'loose yourself', but, when you do 'get back to yourself'... strengthen your brethren! ■

An Invitation to Study Bible
Thursdays. 6:30 pm
mustardseedfaith@bellsouth.net

January 30, 2009

Faith of a mustard seed
by Barbara Woods-Washington, M. Div.

Before moving on to John's Gospel an interlude from the heart and pen of Howard Thurman is always in order. From **'The Inward Journey'** he entitles this writing **'The Triumphant Entry'**.

"Searching indeed must have been the thoughts moving through the mind of the Master as he jogged along on the back of the donkey on that fateful day which marks in the Christian calendar the Triumphant Entry. The experience must have been as strange and out of character for him as it was for the faithful animal on whose back he rode.

For more than two years, Jesus had been engaged in a public ministry. Once when there were those who wanted to make him a king, he had refused. "My kingdom is not of this world." He had walked the countryside with his band of disciples, preaching, teaching,

Barbara Woods Riles Washington

healing and spreading a quality of radiance that could come only from one whose overwhelming enthusiasm was for God and His Kingdom. He had kept many lonely trysts in the late watches of the night, trueing his spirit and his whole life by the will of his Father. So close had he worked with God that the line of demarcation between his will and God's Will would fade and reappear, fade and reappear. Step by resolute step, he had come to the great city. Deep within his spirit there may have been a sense of foreboding, or the heightened quality of exhilaration that comes from knowing that there is no road back.

He had learned much. So sensitive had grown his spirit and the living quality of his being that he seemed more and more to stand inside of life,

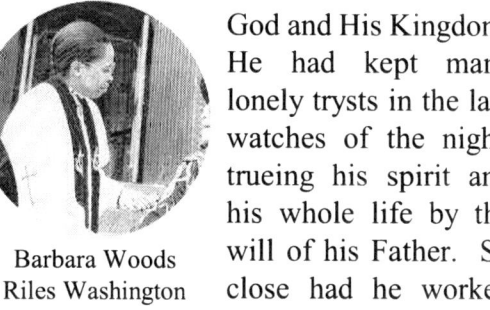

"The Voice Of A Proud Community"
Nashville P*R*I*D*E
Pulpit, Pew and Public

☦ 99

looking out upon it as a man who gazes from a window in a room out into the yard and beyond to the distant hills. He could feel the sparrowness of the sparrow, the leprosy of the leper, the blindness of the blind, the crippleness of the cripple, and the frenzy of the mad. He had become joy, sorrow, hope, anguish, to the joyful, the sorrowful, the hopeful, the anguished. Could he feel his way into the mind and the mood of those who cast the palms and flowers in his path? Was he in the cry of those who exclaimed their wild and unrestrained Hosannas? Did he mingle with the emotions that lay beneath the exultations ready to explode in the outburst of the mob screaming, "Crucify him! Crucify him!" I wonder what was at work in the mind of Jesus of Nazareth as he jogged along on the back of the faithful donkey.

Perhaps his mind was far away to the scenes of his childhood, feeling the sawdust between his toes, in his father's shop. He may have been remembering the high holy days in the synagogue, with his whole body quickened by the echo of the ram's horn as it sounded. Or perhaps he was thinking of his mother, how deeply he loved her and how he wished that there had not been laid upon him the Great Necessity which sent him out on the open road to proclaim the Truth, leaving her side forever. It may be that he lived all over again that high moment on the Sabbath when he was handed the scroll and he unrolled it to the great passage from the prophet Isaiah, *"The spirit of the Lord is upon me, for he has anointed me to preach the gospel to the poor, to open the eyes of the blind, to unstop the ears of the deaf, to announce the acceptable year of the Lord."* I wonder what was moving through the mind of the Master as he jogged along on the back of the faithful donkey."■

An Invitation to Study Bible Thursdays. 6:30 pm mustardseedfaith@bellsouth.net

_____
February 6, 2009
_____

Faith of a mustard seed
by Barbara Woods-Washington, M. Div.

The writings of Dr. Howard Thurman are so universal in interpretation that it is unjust to do so in written context. For this reason I commend it to you in original text. As he would say to us " you put a handle on it." As an introduction to Christianity as a world religion I included this text from **'Jesus And The Disinherited'** as part of the work in my **'Philosophy of Religion'** course at Bennett College. A fitting contribution to Black History month study.

In the fall of 1935 I was serving as chairman of a delegation sent on a pilgrimage of friendship from the students of America to the students of India, Burma, and Ceylon. It was at a meeting in Ceylon that the whole crucial issue was pointed up to me in a way that I can never forget. At the close of a talk before the Law College, University of Colombo, on civil disabilities under states' rights in the United States, I was invited by the principal to have coffee.

We drank our coffee in silence. After the service had been removed, he said to me, "What are you doing over here? I know what the newspapers say about a pilgrimage of friendship and the rest, but that is not my question. What are *you* doing over here? This is what I mean.

More than three hundred years ago your forefathers were taken from the western coast of Africa as slaves. The people who dealt in the slave traffic were Christians. One of your famous Christian hymn writers, Sir John Newton, made his money from the sale of slaves to the New World. He is the man who wrote, 'How Sweet the Name of Jesus Sounds' and 'Amazing Grace'— there may be others, but these are the only

Barbara Woods Riles Washington

ones I know. The name of one of the famous British slave vessels was 'Jesus.'

The men who bought the slaves were Christians. Christian ministers, quoting the Christian apostle Paul, gave the sanction of religion to the system of slavery. Some seventy years or more ago you were freed by a man who was not a professing Christian, but was rather the spearhead of certain political, social, and economic forces, the significance of which he himself did not understand. During all the period since then you have lived in a Christian nation in which you are segregated, lynched, and burned. Even in the church, I understand, there is segregation. One of my students who went to your country sent me a clipping telling about a Christian church in which the regular Sunday worship was interrupted so that many could join in a mob against one of your fellows. When he had been caught and done to death, they came back to resume their worship of their Christian God.

I am a Hundu. I do not understand. Here you are in my country, standing deep within the Christian faith and tradition. I do not wish to seem rude to you, But, sir, I think you are a traitor to all the darker peoples of the earth. I am wondering what you, an intelligent man, can say in defense of your position."

With this encounter as a catalyst, Dr. Thurman then writes, "It is a privilege, after so long a time, to set down what seems to me to be an essentially creative and prognostic interpretation of Jesus as religious subject rather than religious object."

This book was required reading in preparation for and became the central text of our Seven Day Intensive Study with him on The Grounds and Meaning of Religious Experience. ■

An Invitation to Study Bible Thursdays. 6:30 pm mustardseedfaith@bellsouth.net

_____
February 13, 2009
_____

Faith of a mustard seed
by Barbara Woods-Washington, M. Div.

Moving to John's Gospel and it's use of 'pistis/faith' reveals a significant note in that our resource, Young's Analytical Concordance to Bible, has identified no uses of 'pistis' in John's Gospel. The hows and whys might lead us further into the work that New Testament scholars have accomplished in seeing and separating the Three **'Synoptic Gospels'** (Matthew, Mark and Luke) from the 4th Gospel, John.

Having viewed the separate and individual uses of 'pistis/faith' in each of the Synoptics, the question can now be raised, 'what does these three Gospels say concerning 'pistis/faith'? So glad you asked! Because it makes us see a Word of Faith that is found EXCLUSIVELY IN JESUS!

Matthew tells it this way:
"Truly, I say to you, not even in Israel have I found such faith!"

Barbara Woods Riles Washington

"Take heart, daughter, your faith has made you well."
"According to your faith let it be done to you."
"O woman, great is your faith! be it done for you as you desire."
"O faithless and perverse generation, how long am I to be with you?"
"Because of your little faith. For truly I tell you, if you have faith as a grain of mustard seed, you will say to this mountain, 'move hence to yonder place,' and it will move; and nothing will be impossible to you."
"Truly I tell you, if you have faith and never doubt, you will not only do what has been done to the fig tree, but even if you say to this mountain, 'be taken up and cast into the sea,' it will be done. And whatever you ask in prayer, you will receive, if you have faith."

The Voice Of A Proud Community
Nashville P*R*I*D*E
Pulpit, Pew and Public

☦ 103

"Woe to you, scribes and Pharisees, hypocrites! for you tithe mint, dill, and cummin, and have neglected the weightier matters of the law; justice and mercy and faith;"

Mark tells it like this:
"Why are you afraid? Have you no faith?"
"Daughter, your faith has made you well; go in peace, and be healed of your disease."
"Go your way; your faith has made you well."
"Have faith in God."

Luke speaks to say:
"I tell you, not even in Israel have I found such faith!"
"Your faith has saved you; go in peace."
"Where is your faith?"
"Daughter, your faith has made you well; go in peace."
"If you had faith as a grain of mustard seed, you could say to this sycamine tree, 'Be rooted up, and be planted in the sea', and it would obey you."
"Rise and go your way; your faith has made you well."

"Nevertheless, when the Son of man comes, will he find faith on earth?"
"Receive your sight; your faith has made you well."
"But I have prayed for you that your faith may not fail;"

Where **John** is silent.

A single exception to Jesus' Spoken Word Faith is the disciples plea, *"Increase our faith!"* Luke is the only one who knew about this. (All by itself— this will preach! I wish I had a praying Church!)

Beyond this Word of Faith Spoken by Jesus, there is the occurrence that all three Synoptic writers record on the occasion of **'The Healing of The Paralytic'**. On this day, Jesus SEES FAITH! In this man's friends. Their brother's keeper. Which prompts him to speak this Word on: FORGIVENESS OF SIN!■

*An Invitation to Study Bible
Thursdays, 6:30 pm
mustardseedfaith@bellsouth.net*

March 6, 2009

PS

"The Voice of a Proud Community"
NASHVILLE PRIDE

Faith of a mustard seed

By Barbara A. Woods Washington, M. Div.

"But Felix, having a rather accurate knowledge of the Way, put them off, saying, "When' Lysias the tribune comes down, I will decide your case." Then he gave orders to the centurion that he (Paul) be kept in custody but should have some liberty, and that none of his friends should be prevented from attending to his needs.

After some days Felix came and his wife Drusilla, who is a Jewess; and he sent for Paul and heard him speak upon faith in Christ Jesus.", (Acts 24:22-24). The 11th occurrence of 'pistis/faith' in the Acts of The Apostles.

The testing of Paul's faith from his testimony of the previous 10th occurrence of 'pistis/faith' in Acts is fraught with life and death defense. Since his 'Farewell Speech' given to the Elders of Ephesus he has stopped in Tyre where not only the disciples there, but the Judean ecstatic Agabus warns Paul not to go to Jerusalem for, "so shall the Jews at Jerusalem bind the man who owns this belt and deliver him into the hands of the Gentiles.".

The question of 'The Law.' is still not settled in Jerusalem. 'The Way — the church' is even further still from securing it's own identity as it continues a defining struggle inside Judaism. James, now in leadership assembled the elders to receive Paul upon his arrival. He, too, still loyal to 'The Law' fears for Paul's life as they devise a plan: "take these men and purify yourself along with them and pay their expenses, so that they may shave their heads. Thus all will know that there is nothing in what they have been told about you but you yourself live in observance to the law.."

Can't exactly put my hands on the whys of Paul following this plan devised by man, particularly when he 'is' in my thinking of the original recipient of The Holy Spirit. I know, I know, we can debate Pentecost, but it is Paul (not the Twelve) who 'Christ(alizes)'; 'Christ(olo-gizes)' and gives meaning and definition to having received the personal gift of the Holy Spirit through his Damascus experience. And the use, 'Paul's use' of spiritual gifts in giving incarnation to the power of the spirit of Christ; but, while at the Temple following James and the Jerusalem elders' plan, he is seized, dragged from the Temple and the violence upon his life begins anew.

In all of this the 'Who I Am' of Paul emerges into the brightest of lights. We have come upon the 2nd recording of his 'conversion'; but now in 1st person. He asks the tribune to allow him to speak to the mob that has called for his detainment and in Hebrew he says, "I am a Jew, born at Tarsus in Cilicia, but brought up in this city at the feet of Gamaliel, educated according to the strict manner of the law of our fathers, being zealous for God as you all are this day..." Before this 'Speech From The Steps Of The Fortress' in Jerusalem is concluded he reminds them of how he persecuted this 'way' delivering them to prison, even carrying letters from the high priest and the whole presbytery as license for this mission of death and destruction. The final response of the mob: "Away with such a man from the earth! For it is not right that he should live."

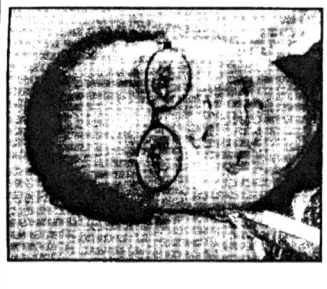

It is Jesus who reminds us that a prophet is not without honor, except in his own home. Paul is home and the violence against his life has reached it's peak. His own people have now decided that it is time for him to die. Must note before leaving this space that his only relative identified enters here; his nephew comes to him where he is being held to warn him of the assassination 'curse' plot that has been set in motion.

Follow me on Twitter @therevsquilts

mustardseedfaith@bellsouth.net

Barbara A. Woods Washington

August 17, 2012 www.pridepublishinggroup.com **Pulpit, Pew & Public** Nashville PRIDE

xii

NASHVILLE P✦R✦I✦D✦E

The Voice of a Proud Community

| Headlines | Local News | Our Times | Church | Editorials | Leisure & Sports | Calendar | People | Archives |

RECENT STORIES

- Governor unveils 'Tennessee Promise' Free community and technology college education proposed
- The story that must be told Crisis grows for young black men, but have we had enough?
- Power of 12 Seahawks crush the Broncos in Super Bowl
- Profiles in excellence Team USA Olympic athletes at Sochi Winter Games
- Nashville's Southern Women's Show — A 'festival of fun' to be held

RECENT COMMENTS

PRIDE Newsdesk on Marvel's Iron Man 3 rockets into the record books
daphne79 on Nashville Film Festival returns
luciless on Nashville Film Festival returns

Faith of a mustard seed

June 14, 2013

By Barbara A. Woods Washington, M. Div.

Both Ernest Kasemann and Joseph Fitzmyer have identified in their 'Commentaries on Romans' the text of 3:21-31 as THE THESIS of this Book. The magnitude of this reveals to me that if I can 'get this', 'see this', 'understand this' — then I will have seriously, critically 'increased my faith'; the prayer that every Christian should pray— daily!

Helpful, then, is the division that Fitzmyer has used in dividing the 'Thesis' statement of Romans into two parts: 1) verses 3:21-26 and, 2) verses 3:27-31. Therefore, again, again, and yet again:

"But now the righteousness of God has been manifested apart from law, although the law and the prophets bear witness to it; the righteousness of God through faith in Jesus Christ for all who believe. For there is no distinction; since all have sinned and fall short of the glory of God; they are justified by his grace as a gift, through the redemption which is in Christ Jesus, whom God put forward as an expiation by his blood, to be received by faith. This was to show God's

Barbara A. Woods-Washington

righteousness, because in his divine forbearance he had passed over former sins; it was to prove at the present time that he himself is righteous and that he justifies him who has faith in Jesus." (Romans 3:21-26) with 4 occurrences of 'pistis/faith'.

Running the numbers again, so useful. These four words that Paul uses more than 60-70 times EACH in this Letter/Book, look, they are all here in just these Six (6) verses: righteousness (4 times), faith (4 times) law (2 times); and sin (2 times).

Alas, we have reached a time in this Empire— these United States of America, when 'The Law' has been exposed for the 'demigod' that it is. I know, I know, some of you are thinking that now 'she has lost her mind'! But, I assure you that this is something that 'flesh and blood' CANNOT REVEAL to you. "But now THE RIGHTEOUSNESS OF GOD has been MANIFESTED APART FROM LAW…," God has shown 'Godself' (power, majesty, dominion, sovereignty, salvation… APART (Turn to your neighbor and say APART! Webster! separately; as regards place and time; in consideration or function; independently; disassociated;…) from LAW (man-power, man-majesty, man-dominion, man-made sovereignty) 'Only as contradiction…"

Again, run THESE numbers: It has come to pass that the office of the President of the United States, which now requires not less than a Billion Dollars to have and to hold — is a lawyer. The First Lady is a lawyer. Count the number of United States Senators (and Tennessee State Senators for this matter) who are lawyers. Inventory the number of Houses of Representatives (both national and pick a state, any state) members who are lawyers. The Judges! The Lobbyist on whom so much is being written now about the 'revolving door' between 'The Chamber' and 'The Lobby' — oh yeah, all Lawyers! Thank you God, thank you Paul for this revelation: "But now the righteousness (justice) of God has been manifested apart from (disassociated with) law…"

Follow me on Twitter: @thereyouquilts or e-mail, mustardseed@abaa-bellsouth.net

xiii www.pridepublishinggroup.com

CPSIA information can be obtained at www.ICGtesting.com
Printed in the USA
LVOW10s1154220115

423902LV00003B/4/P